BANDS ON THE ROAD

BANDS ON THE ROAD
The Tour Sketchbook

Silke Leicher & Manuel Schreiner

with 304 color illustrations

On the cover: "Bob the Bass Tech" by Markka Lappalainen of Hoobastank (see page 118)

All drawings and sketches were created exclusively for this book.

Exclusively licensed from edel entertainment GmbH/Rockbuch, Germany.

Original edition © 2006 Rockbuch Verlag Buhmann & Haeseler GmbH, Schlüchtern
English edition © 2008 Thames & Hudson Ltd, London

First published in 2008 in the United States of America by Thames & Hudson Inc., 500 Fifth Avenue, New York, New York 10110

thamesandhudsonusa.com

Library of Congress Catalog Card Number 2008901881

ISBN 978-0-500-28773-6

Printed and bound in China by C&C Offset Printing Co., Ltd

CONTENTS

FOREWORD

Any sort of travel can change your perception of things.
Time becomes altogether more stretched or compact, depending
on the environment or the commitments you have made. Life on
tour could so easily pass without incident. Musicians have so
many people working on their behalf so that they only need to
concentrate on performances. But, rather than allow the world
to escape, it's better to break free of the bubble and stir
dormant thoughts.

This book displays the preoccupations of people on tour. Some
contributions are flippant and some are more considered. Both
approaches have their merits and help give an insight into the
personalites of the artist. Any type of mark-making stems from
a primal impulse and readers will probably be searching for
clues about the person behind the drawing.

I have seen so many incredible sights during the last year or so.
It makes sense to me to convert some of those experiences into
a drawing. I suppose it's a celebration, or, at least, a document.

There are lots of illustrations in this book that were done quickly
and with a sense of humour, indicating the transient quality of life
on the move. Sometimes it's better to forget home and enjoy the
moment. Equally, there is comfort in thoughts (and consequently
pictures) of where you come from or places and people that fill
your head with pleasant dreams. I hope these offerings give you
a small insight into lives being lived.

PAUL SMITH
MAXÏMO PARK

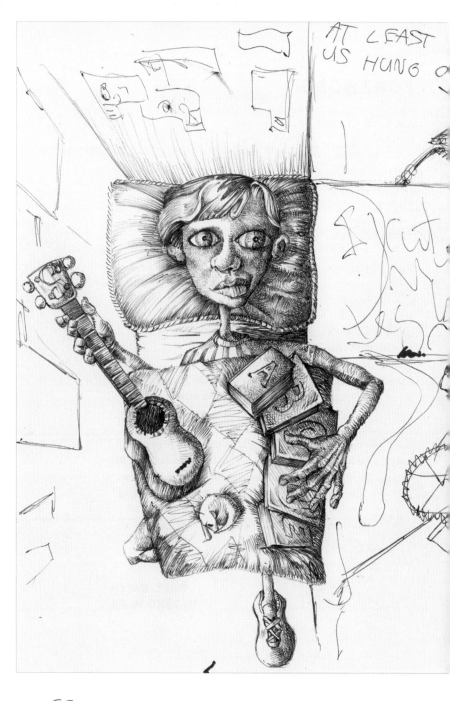

66 On the left is me in my bedroom. That's where I did most of my songwriting... **99**

>> 222

DELAYS/
GREG GILBERT
Childhood Memory

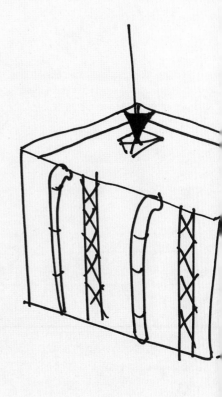

❝ I can just remember the door closing
and me being stuck out there... ❞

>> 223

I found my way out
of the pompidou
centre here.

COLDPLAY/
GUY BERRYMAN

The Pompidou Centre, Paris

66 I grew up in downtown Manhattan,
so that's the universe to me... 99

>> 223

JEFF LEWIS Lower EAST SIDE DRAWING

JEFFREY
LEWIS
Lower East Side

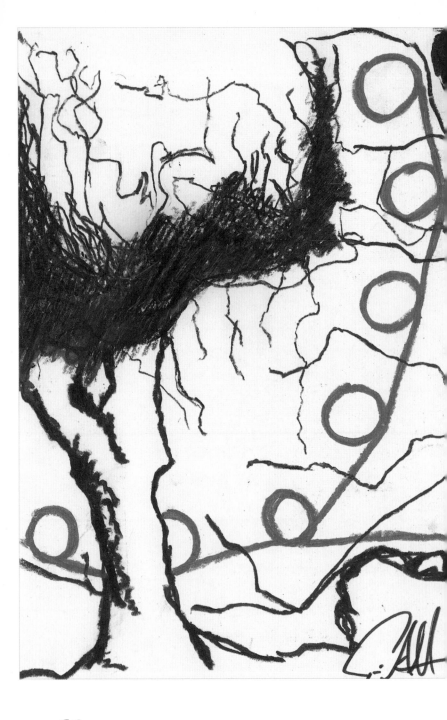

>> 224

66 I have no idea what we intended to
do with all those bikes... 99

THE USED/
QUINN ALLMAN

Stealing Bikes

>> 225

FAN ATTACKS DANIEL IN JAPAN AT FUJI ROCK FESTIVAL (APART FROM THAT WE ALWAYS HAD A BEAUTIFUL TIME IN A UNIQUE COUNTRY!)

THE THRILLS/
CONOR DEASY

Attack by a Japanese Fan

"NEON

It's not just a Japanese cultural icon...It represents showing the monster side...

>> 225

FEEDER/
GRANT NICHOLAS
Godzilla

66 Once upon a time there was a chameleon... 99

>> 226

FUCK/
KYLE DARIN STATHAM
Ice Cream Shop in Frankfurt

66 This steady place reminds me how
things keep changing in life... 99

>> 227

24

There is a hill on the south
side of Glasgow where I go
to have some peace. You can
see the city and beyond from
this vantage point. I have
known of this place since I
was 12 years old. There is a
little monument that I lean
my back against. There is a
plaque beside the monument
that says Mary Queen of
Scots stood at the very same
point and watched her army
being defeated in the 1600's
██████████ I wrote a song called
'walking down the hill' about
this place. The best time to
go to the hill is in autum,
and winter when the leaves
have gone.

TRAVIS/
FRAN HEALY

Hill in Glasgow

The Crash in Aust

66 We were almost trapped in the mountains because we couldn't find the place where we had left our car... 99

>> 227

THE CRASH/
TEEMU BRUNILA

Four Finns in Austria

there is Company
in every breath
I take

>> 228

**IDLEWILD/
RODDY WOOMBLE**
House in the Scottish Highlands

❝ I can't ever remember a time when I didn't play... ❞

>> 229

by

Matt Hales
31/3/2005

AQUALUNG/
MATT HALES
First Piano

31

" Do I really have to say what was so important about it? It was my bedroom... **"**

>> 230

ADAM
GREEN

My Room

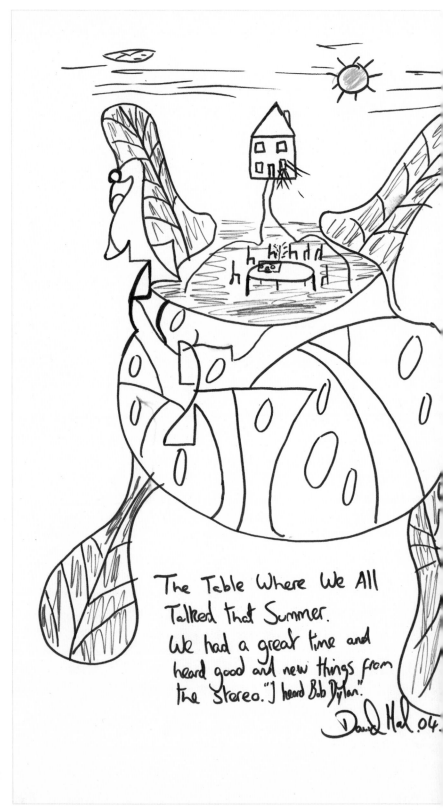

The Table Where We All Talked that Summer.
We had a great time and heard good and new things from the Stereo. "I heard Bob Dylan".

David Mal. 04.

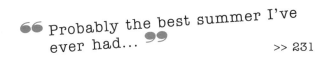

66 Probably the best summer I've ever had... 99

>> 231

HAL/
DAVID ALLEN
Table in the Garden

66 You're always looking for somebody.
That's the painful side of it... 99

>> 231

MONEYBROTHER/ ANDERS WENDIN
Nobody's Lonely Tonight

> 66 It was easy to remember which was the right road for the shop, because there was a clock at the end of it... 99

>> 232

ART BRUT/
EDDIE ARGOS
Joke Shop

66 I remember watching the lions for about two hours... 99

>> 232

THE CORAL/
JOHN DUFFY

The Zoo

“It was a whole weekend, listening to music and dancing...”

>> 233

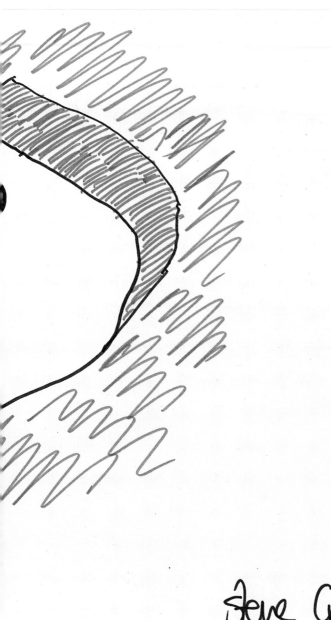

Steve Cradock.
ocean colour Scene

OCEAN COLOUR SCENE/
STEVE CRADOCK
Scooter Festival, Isle of Wight

"Adream" circa 1976

Interpol

66 Probably my best memory...I guess it makes no difference that it was created by my subconscious... 99

>> 234

I must have been 8 or 9 years of age the first time I was brought to what will later become more than just a favorite place. A small wooden cubical - old and beaten, but not with out a powerful charm. Seemingly, this rustic shack was used to print a news paper, or something of the like. An old woman was the "press op." She spoke not a word - verbal, But she made me feel safe and secure. In the company of the press operator, nothing could be of harm. Without a touch, she held me close and kept me warm. I would stand in the corner for hours under dim light and watch her work under dim light... I still visit her from time to time - when all is right or wrong. I still look to her for safety, and she gives it to me sans words while she prints the words of others...

INTERPOL/
SAMUEL FOGARINO
A Dream of Philadelphia

heartbreaking moment of me finding out that they had cut down my favourite tree where I used to sit for hours

66 I felt like I had lost a friend...99

>> 235

THE CAESARS/
DAVID LINDQUIST
Dead Tree

" It's kind of depressing and funny at the same time... **"**

>> 235

THE CAESARS/
CÉSAR VIDAL

Sheffield

THIS I[...]
FAMLY WOULD [...]
MUM & DAD'S HAUS (ALTHUGH I D[...]
DONE IT). COS WE R AWAY FROM HOME H'[...]

> " It's not the kind of thing you think
> of as a dream job for your kid, is it? "

>> 236

DIRTY PRETTY THINGS &
THE COOPER TEMPLE CLAUSE/
DIDZ HAMMOND

House & Family

“ They were really cute, but also terrors! ”

>> 236

WE ARE SCIENTISTS/
MICHAEL TAPPER

Kittens

It was one of the first times in my
life that a dream became a reality...

>> 237

LIFE OF AGONY/
ALAN ROBERT
Sad Way Home

66 I had really good parties and got to be the boss of the house! 99

>> 238

FRANZ FERDINAND/
BOB HARDY
My Parents' House

“At the table I learned to make ravioli and gnocchi...”

>> 239

CRISTINA
DONÀ
Grandmother's Kitchen

66 I was twelve years old when I wrote
my first real song. It was terrible! 99

>> 240

Nov 30, 2004

THE DRESDEN DOLLS/
AMANDA PALMER
On the Piano

66 This is my earliest memory. I was one year old... 99 >> 240

MUSE/
DOMINIC HOWARD

Baby on Board

❝ I felt like I was exactly where I wanted to be at that time... ❞

>> 241

64

THE DRESDEN DOLLS/
BRIAN VIGLIONE

My Room When I Was 18

66 I got a lot of inspiration from that place! 99

>> 242

STEREOPHONICS/
KELLY JONES

Market Trader

" I used to go there with my parents every weekend... **"**

>> 242

Matthew Caws, Nada Surf

NADA SURF/
MATTHEW CAWS
Central Park

66 Beaches fascinate me, every single grain of sand... **99**

>> 243

JJ72/
MARK GREANEY

Dublin Coast

66 I've drawn the hospital where my first child was born... 99

>> 244

ATHLETE/
JOEL POTT
Birth of My Daughter

THE BIRTH BY [signature] (Stars

66 I sat up all night by the side of the
bed where my girlfriend was... 99
>> 244

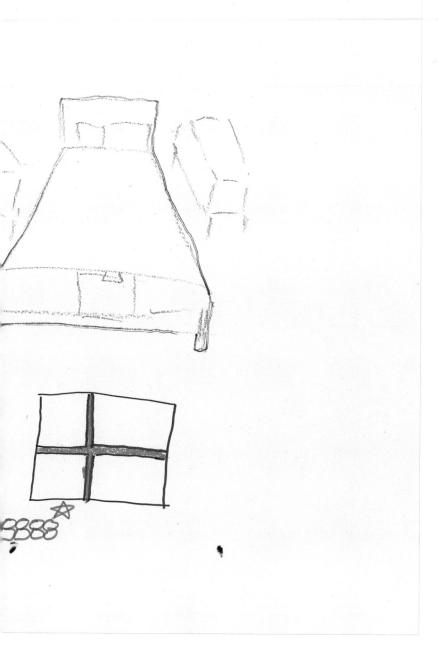

**STARSAILOR/
JAMES WALSH**
The Birth

66 It feels like you aren't just hearing the music with your head, but with your whole body... 99

>> 245

2RAUMWOHNUNG/
TOMMI ECKART

Stereo

66 That's the view from behind the wheels of steel... 99

>> 246

BELLE AND SEBASTIAN/
CHRIS GEDDES

DJ Night in Glasgow

> **❝** I sometimes go there to get crazy or to relax...but mostly to get crazy, I think... **❞**

>> 247

OASIS/
NOEL GALLAGHER
Ibiza Smiley

66 You feel like you've lost a little bit of your youth, but it is very exciting... 99

>> 248

KAISER CHIEFS/
RICKY WILSON
House in Leeds

Battle Abbe

66 I'm afraid the drawing doesn't really
do it justice... 99

>> 249

by Richard
KEANE
age 28 1066

ps I am colourblind.

KEANE/
RICHARD HUGHES
Battle Abbey

**   **It feels like I'm travelling in a kind of bubble that I never really get out of... **"**

>> 250

As a kid, I used to have a fasicination with old scandinavian culture (Vikings). I also had a love of water and ships and sailing etc. Anything that had to do with traveling. So now twenty years later and touring the world this is the closest thing that I can explain to people how touring life is. We are in a constant traveling bubble. In a sorts, like adventurers going to different lands and being on the ~~fringes of~~ normal society. Of course no one travels by boat but this is the closest analogy that I can explain with ~~their~~ and my friends and family can kind of relate but, I guess until someone has experienced it the only real way to see it. It may be a bit romanticized but that is what I feel about it. It excites me when we start a new tour and I cherish all the places and people we have met along the way.

SPARTA/
MATT MILLER
Ship

On the road, I have
bus. When you go scu[
without an air tank. I
You do not go on the
If I knew 
have to spend
my life with one woman,
woman now, I would cho
this just in case the perso
count the bus as a woman
me if I were to choose

66 Without it, touring is a waking nightmare... 99

>> 250

t one friend: the
living, you do not go
you do, you will die.
without a bus.
that I would
the rest of
I had to choose that
the bus. I would do
king the rules might
take the bus away from
abeth.

We Are Scientists

WE ARE SCIENTISTS/
CHRIS CAIN

Mineshaft Canary

66 If you think you are just going to be a rock'n'roll star and everything is just stars and glamour, you couldn't make it through the day... 99

>> 251

ESKOBAR/
ROBERT BIRMING &
FREDERIK ZÄLL

Tour Bus

There's plenty of toilet paper and a very efficient curtain, so that no one can see in...

>> 252

NEED ON TOUR.
TURED   Nick Kaiser Chiefs.

KAISER CHIEFS/
NICK HODGSON
Toilet

93

66 When I think of that moment, I can
still feel the shock... 99

>> 252

THE CAESARS/
NINO KELLER

Traffic Accident

66 I was impressed by the attempts of all the performers to create an effect... 99

>> 253

FUCK/
GEOFFREY HAROLD SOUL
Small Town Magic Show

66 I wish I could be down there in the crowd, looking at the five of us at the same time... 99

>> 254

THE HIVES/
CHRIS DANGEROUS

From the Drummer's Point of View

66 It was just one of those moments, me and my girlfriend were really loved up... 99

>> 254

OCEANSIZE/
MIKE VENNART

Stoned at Glastonbury,
Watching Travis

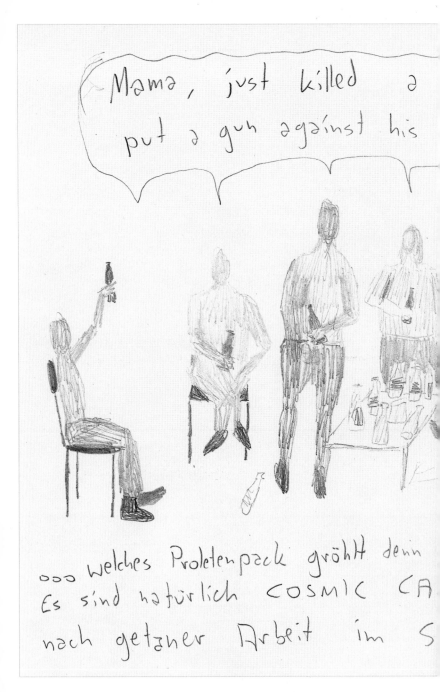

COSMIC CASINO/
MESS
Bohemian Rhapsody

Backstage : Köln - The Never Ending Client

Client B
xXx

❝On days like this, there are still
some surprises left...❞
>> 256

CLIENT/
CLIENT B

Backstage in Cologne

>> 257

66 That was the first time I really realized that our songs could touch someone... 99

THE VON BONDIES/
JASON STOLLSTEIMER

Polaroid

BACKSTAGE A
THERE WAS
MADE FOR T
AND EX-GIR
FEELING A
THE PIXIES

THE

Gordy8
BLOC PARTY.

66 We have played some really nice tours but you don't often get a chance to sit and relax... 99

>> 257

MERRIWEATHER PAVILION, WASHINGTON D.C.
E ARTIST'S GARDEN. I LAY ON A HAMMOCK
MY GIRLFRIEND. WE TALKED ABOUT EX-BOYFRIENDS
S. WE WERE OPENING FOR THE PIXIES AND
AY BECAUSE WE WERE DRINKING BEER AND
LLOW BEER BACKSTAGE...

E SOME CANADA GEESE AND BABY GOSLINGS.

BLOC PARTY/
GORDON MOAKES

Backstage Idyll

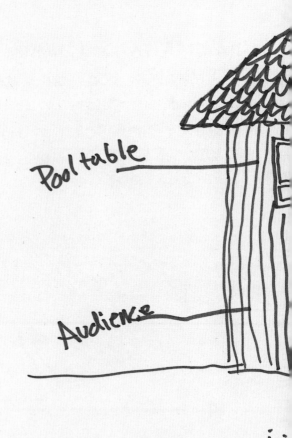

Pool table

Audience

By Gus

66 This is our first rehearsal place. Even Jimi Hendrix has been there... 99

>> 258

Guitars
Drums

RPET

rén in MANDO DIAO

MANDO DIAO/
GUSTAF NORÉN

Shed

" This is where we spend most time together... **""**

>> 25

TELE/
MARTIN BROMBACHER

Rehearsal Room

It looks like Motown or Abbey Road in 1964 in a weird way... >> 259

LOUIS XIV/
JASON HILL
Recording Studio

" Something that could have been horrible was actually a blessing in disguise...**"**

>> 260

THE SHINS/
MARTY CRANDALL

Rehearsal Room

“We needed a bass tech, so our tour manager stole him from Papa Roach…”
>> 261

HOOBASTANK/
MARKKU LAPPALAINEN
Bob the Bass Tech

While the other kids were riding mountain bikes, I'd be inside the garage, singing and beating on the washer, dryer and refrigerator... “

>> 261

the Garage.

THE KILLERS/
RONNIE VANNUCCI JR

Garage

❝One day we released Victor to the microphone so he could rock...❞

>> 262

SUGARPLUM FAIRY/
CARL NORÉN

First Gig

66 There are bits of fruit just
everywhere... 99   >> 263

THE DATSUNS/
DOLF DE BORST &
PHIL BUSCHKE

Tour Impressions

66 Everyone tried to express and represent some
of the feelings we have when we are on tour...

STARS/
GROUP COLLAGE

Tour Images

66 When I looked out of the window, I saw a completely different landscape... 99

>> 265

DEATH CAB FOR CUTIE/
NICHOLAS HARMER
My View

66 You'll notice that the only person talking is the driver... 99

>> 265

SPEARMINT/
JAMES PARSONS

Inside the Tour Bus

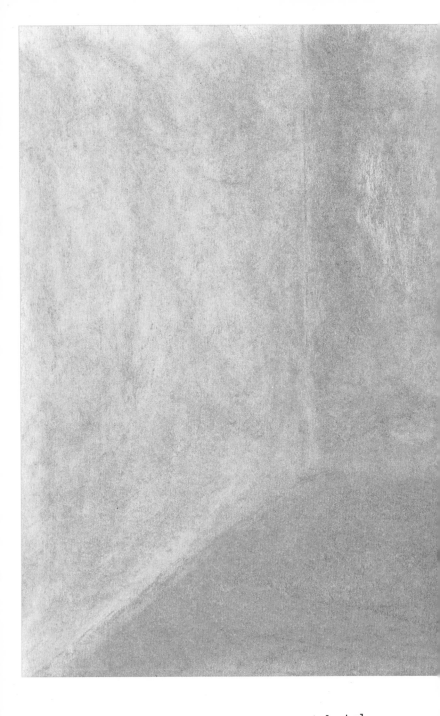

66 We get to see a lot of different hotel rooms, but they all have a similar atmosphere... 99

>> 266

DEATH CAB FOR CUTIE/
CHRIS WALLA
Hotel

"I left something in Moscow"

slum

soldiers

Poe

little bags of bones

Soviet Massive great Dam

66 Every night we did a show and it was always chaos... 99

"I left something in Moscow"

slum

soldiers

Poe

little bags of bones

Soviet Massive great Dam

>> 266

66 Every night we did a show and it was always chaos... 99

BABYSHAMBLES &
THE LIBERTINES/
PETE DOHERTY

Moscow

"As soon as you look up to the roof, it looks like that really dramatic Nazi architecture..."

>> 267

BLACK REBEL
MOTORCYCLE CLUB/
NICK JAGO

Image of the Festhalle

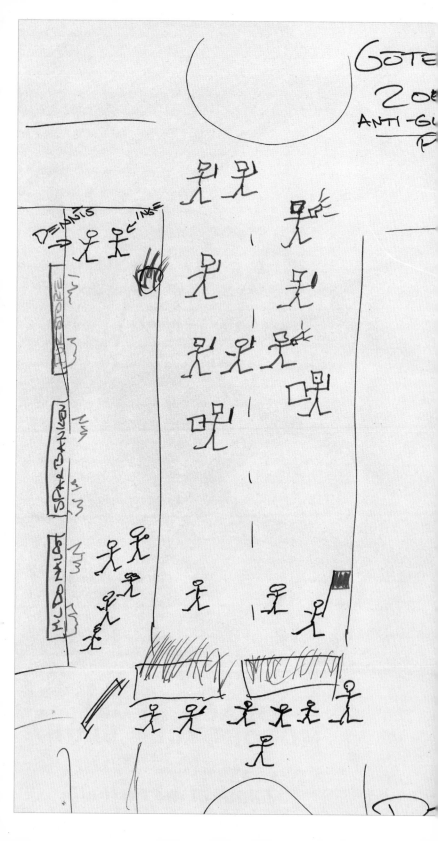

GOTE
20
ANTI-GL
P

DENNIS
INGE

STORE
SPARBANKEN
MCDONALDS

66 When we went back to the studio after everything that had happened, it felt like we had a lot more to say... 99

>> 268

THE
(INTERNATIONAL)
NOISE CONSPIRACY/
DENNIS LYXZÉN

Protest in Gothenburg

66 My last memory of the night before we left is a missile stuck in the top of our apartment building... **99**

>> 269

SPARTA/
TONY HAJJAR
Last Days in Lebanon

>> 270

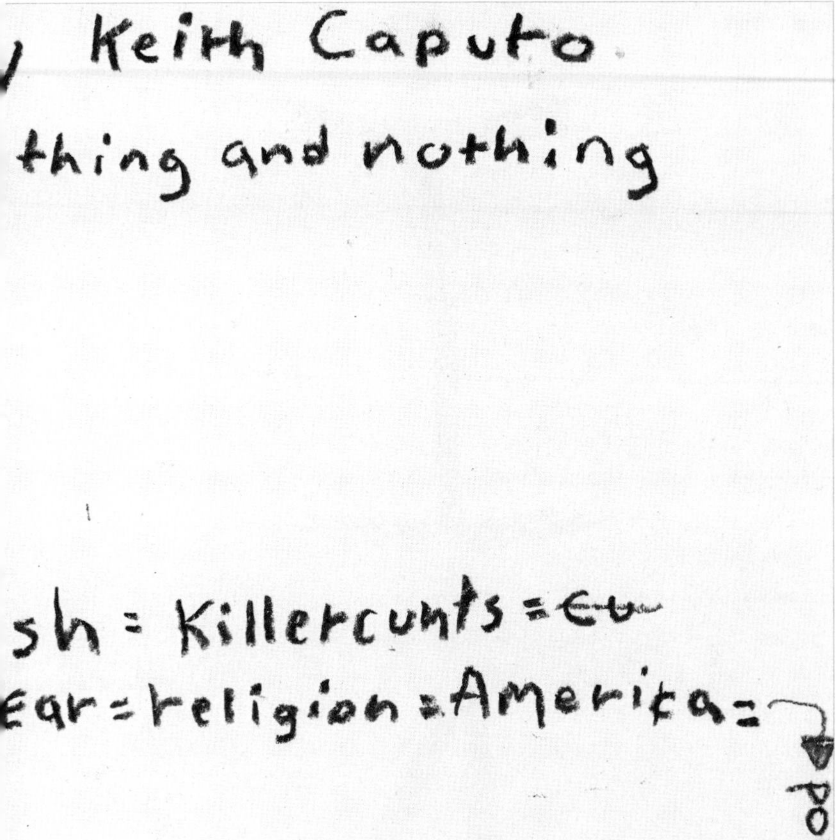

Keith Caputo.

thing and nothing

sh = Killercunts = cu

Ear = religion = America =

power, currency

Blood = greed =

LIFE OF AGONY/
KEITH CAPUTO

September 11

66 I don't know why I have a fascination
with it, a romance... 99

>> 271

SNOW PATROL/
NATHAN CONNOLLY
I Love NY

66 It's all about these monoliths and this imposing stuff and yet there's tremendous freedom artistically... 99

>> 271

I AM KLOOT/
JOHN BRAMWELL

First Time in Berlin

Russian badge bought from street vendor
Moscow January 2005

I fell in love with St Petersburg & Moscow.
The history, the architecture, the literature
The imagery & the world changing Bolshev

Client A.

CLIENT/
CLIENT A
Russian Badge

66 I just find it fascinating that someone decided to pursue such a strange and ambitious project... 99

>> 273

IN LAKE HAVASU, ARIZONA

THE
WEDDING PRESENT/
DAVID GEDGE

London Bridge in Lake Havasu

FARoE ISLANDS
RoUGHLY SKETCHED
BY KEN STRINGFELLOW

66 They look like they were just raised
out of the sea yesterday... 99

>> 274

KEN
STRINGFELLOW
Faroe Islands

66 I woke up that morning understanding that music had the power to bring people together... 99

>> 275

MELISSA
AUF DER MAUR
Dream Desert

Desert = Perception of world
Cube = Perception of self
Stairs = friends
Glass = Love
horse = Desire

❝You ask someone to visualize a desert, a cube, some stairs, a glass and a horse...❞

>> 277

MUSE/
MATTHEW BELLAMY

Psychology Test

PAUL S

❝ It was desolate but I like the emptiness of it...**❞**

>> 27

1st June 2005
Köln

MAXÏMO
PARK.

MAXÏMO PARK/
PAUL SMITH
Cologne Car Park

66 The drawings aren't actually real streets, but made up... 99

>> 278

MAXÏMO PARK/
DUNCAN LLOYD

Cityscape (NYC)

SWAYAM BUNATH   - GREAT

NEPAL

❝ You only have to look at it for
five minutes to be completely
overwhelmed... **❞**

>>279

4/12/02

SLUT/
CHRIS NEUBURGER

The Great Stupa

66 You can feel when you are in tune
with the rhythm with the city... 99

>> 280

PHOENIX/
LAURENT BRANCOWITZ
Tokyo

Five Drums

❝ I've been working on it for about fifteen year
and I don't know how the story will end...❞

>> 280

alcovlers

Conrad Keely 2004

...TRAIL OF DEAD/
CONRAD KEELY

Valeovlers

66 It was the most amazing natural
adrenalin rush ever... **99**

>> 281

THE
DETROIT COBRAS/
RACHEL NAGY

Black Forest

The Reoccuring dream of the pumpin' ghosts...

>> 282

66 I am not really sure if it was a dream or reality... 99

THE SOUNDTRACK OF OUR LIVES/
EBBOT LUNDBERG

A Dream About Ghosts

" Just make up your own interpretation! **"**

>> 283

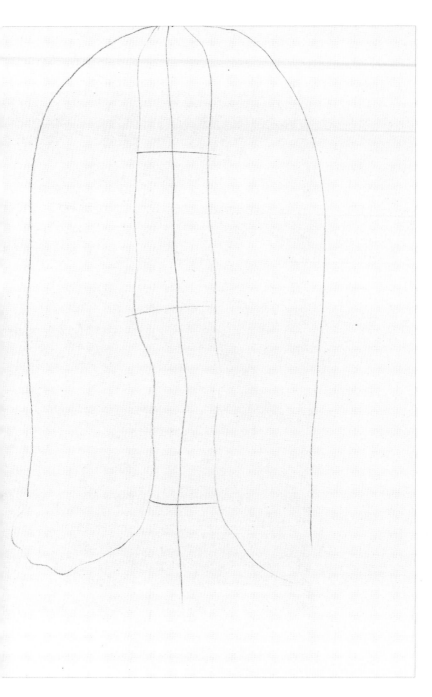

KASABIAN/
CHRIS KARLOFF
Clingfilm Cocoon

Portly Pisscock is a bold young man who gets a lot of pleasure from pissing in a stream...

>> 283

BRITISH SEA POWER/
YAN

Pissing in the Stream

66 What really stayed in my head is the red light district – it's just such an odd place... 99

>> 284

THE RACONTEURS/
BRENDAN BENSON

Amsterdam

66 This is Baltimore! 99

>> 284

DEATH CAB FOR CUTIE/
NICHOLAS HARMER
Baltimore

ADAM WILSON

66 Everyone who visits the wall signs it... 99

>> 284

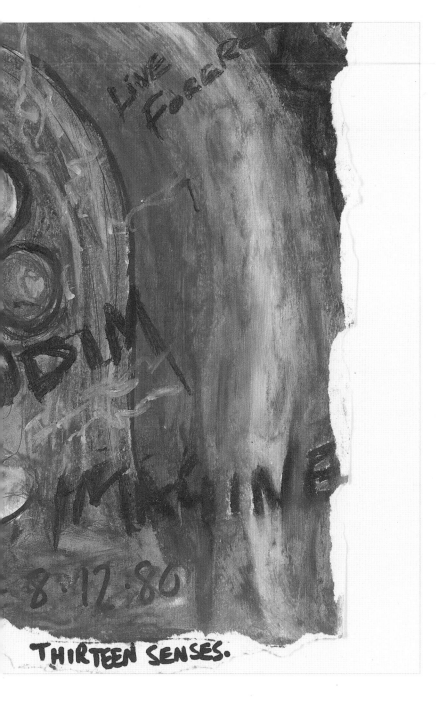

THIRTEEN SENSES/
ADAM WILSON
John Lennon Memorial Wall

66 Now destroyed in the name of progress... **99**

>> 285

MANIC STREET
PREACHERS/
NICKY WIRE

St David's Wood

66 You can wander through underwater tunnels and see sharks, octopuses and tropical fish... 99

>> 286

SNOW PATROL/
MARC McCLELLAND

Aquarium Under the Bridge

66 We got a power boat and just dived into
the lake and swam around all day... 99

>> 286

EMBRACE/
RICHARD McNAMARA
Lake Constance

66 When I feel really down and things are going badly, something beautiful always comes out of it... 99

>> 287

2RAUMWOHNUNG/
INGA HUMPE
Copenhagen Airport

66 Once I was out there for ten days, and didn't speak. It does interesting things to the mind...99

>> 287

**JOHNNY
MARR**

Arizona Desert

" The smell of burning eucalyptus leaves was just amazing... **"**

>> 288

SIMIAN/
ALEX MacNAUGHTON
Holiday in Cyprus

❝ Our manager got a little drunk and decided to take a picture of his own butt... **❞**

**THE FEATURES/
ROLLUM HAAS &
MATT PELHAM**

Bottom Picture

195

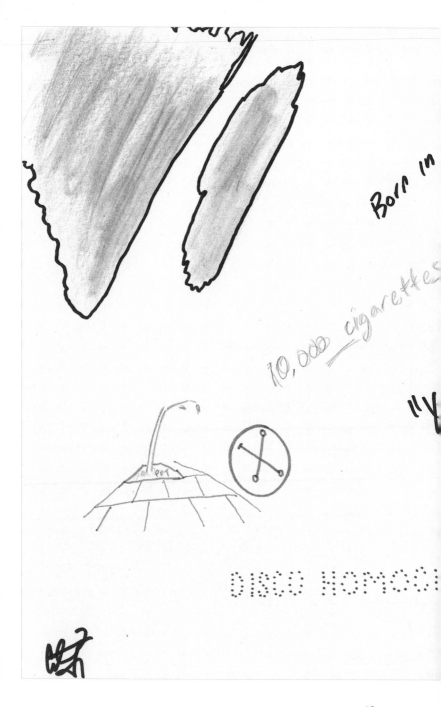

Born in

10,000 cigarettes

DISCO HOMOC

66 I left some pot buried in a sidewalk plant in front of a hotel in Canada... 99

>> 290

thern Italian town of Capra

ened the emporers heart

d "No" closed it

T. V.

THE DANDY WARHOLS/
COURTNEY TAYLOR-TAYLOR
Stoned Impression

Vega 4
JJ
BRYAN
GOOSE
Inside my head
PLAY
LIFE
Knowledge motorway
FREQUENCY
autobahn
nirvana
Boredom
T Rex
DREAMING
DREAMS
VISUAL
questions
MUSIC
Songs
Answers
Shyness
TRAFFIC JAM
led Zeppelin
Radio
Remember
Joni mitchell
Melody
MOVIES
CHAOS!
Radar
IDEAS
WORDS
Peaceful
headache
HABIT
hear
velvet underground
See
SENSATIVITY
smell
SOUL
Big Lebowski
ESCAPISM
suede
Taste
EXCITEMENT
rolling
PANIC
The doors
the strokes
Love
u2
HEALTH
NEWS
COMMUNICATION
GIRLFRIEND
SPECIAL PERSON
FAMILY
david sylvian
watching
Fun
magazines
Fleetwood mac
mum
DAD
BROTHER
SISTER
NAN
MOODY
LIGHT HEARTED
LAUGHTER
Fussy
radiohead
happy?
Smashing Pumpkins
Friends
Space
TALKING
Pulp Fiction
TRAVEL
HANGING OUT
LOSS
up
SEEING
nightime
SEX
daytime
PATIENCE
The STars
caring
INSECURITY
Pornography
I Like the sun
down
GROWING UP
BELIEVING
DREAMS
The moon
sharing
Forgetting
GETTING OLDER
God?
Shopping
PUB CULTURE
Time
WISER
CLOTHES
Paranoia
contradiction
especiall
70'S

66 It's like a big bowl of confusion,
a traffic jam of thoughts and ideas... 99

>>290

VEGA 4/
SIMON WALKER
Thoughts While Touring

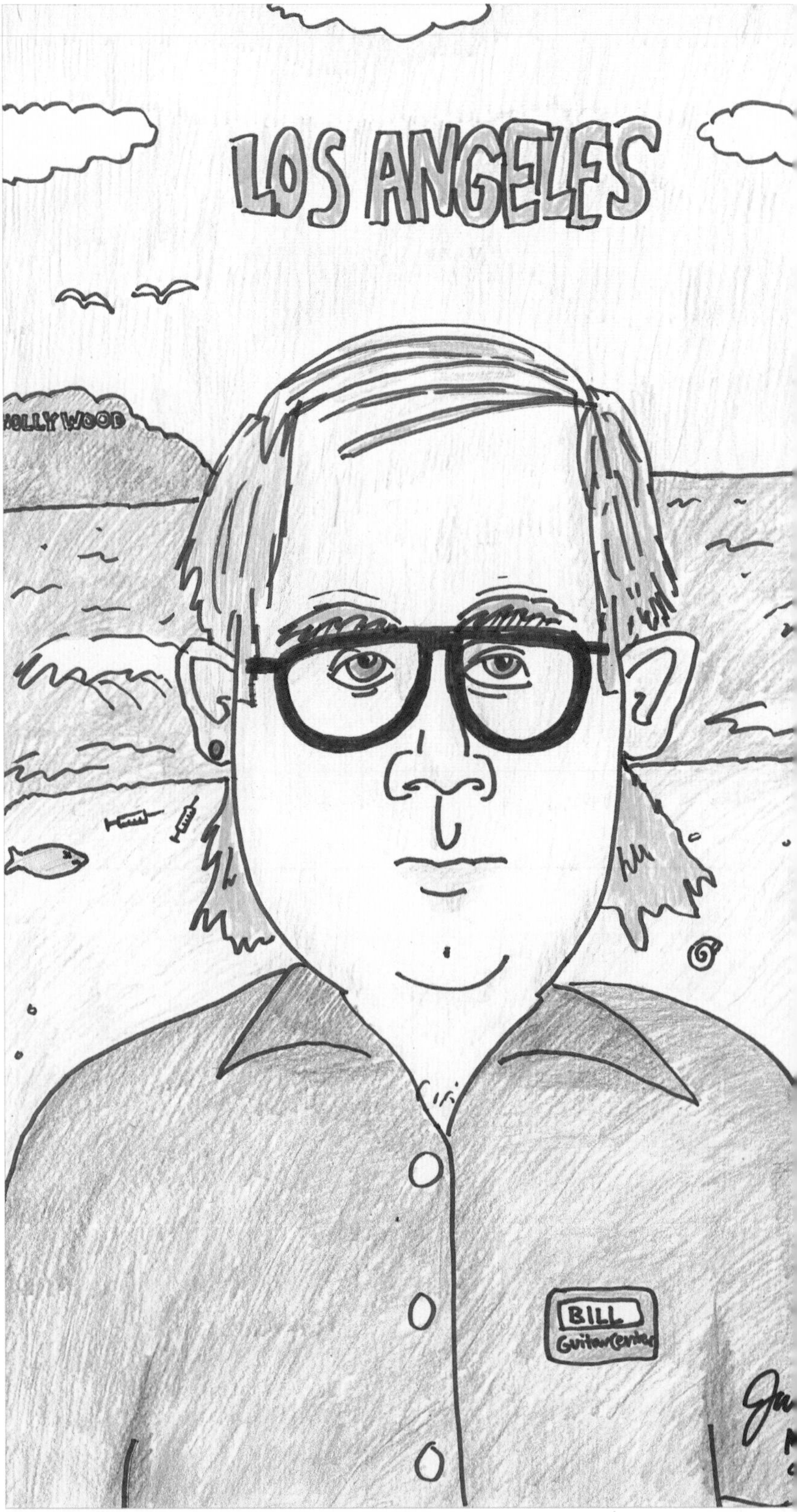
LOS ANGELES
HOLLYWOOD
BILL
GuitarCenter

❝ I don't feel like Bill right now, but I am afraid of becoming him...**❞**

>> 291

MAROON 5/
JAMES VALENTINE
Bill

66 You can see weird little camels roaming
across the picture.... 99

>> 292

WIR SIND HELDEN/
JUDITH HOLOFERNES &
MARK TAVASSOL

Red Telephones

66 While we were playing, the plaster from the ceiling would crumble and fall down around us... 99

>> 293

ASH/
MARK HAMILTON

Rehearsal Shed

THE BASEMENT 1978   QUEENS, N.Y.

"I can't believe that my mom or the neighbours never complained..."

>> 294

NADA SURF/
IRA ELLIOT

Shut Up, Kids!

" We could hear the music through the wall... "

>> 295

THE HIVES/
PELLE ALMQVIST

Rehearsal Room & Disco in Sweden

>> 297

> 66 We thought the place was haunted because weird things happened... 99

THE BLUESKINS/
RYAN SPENDLOVE

Lighthouse

“You can see some trees and rocks and the edge of the lake...and the man in the moon!”

>> 297

HOWIE
DAY
Party at a Lodge in the Woods

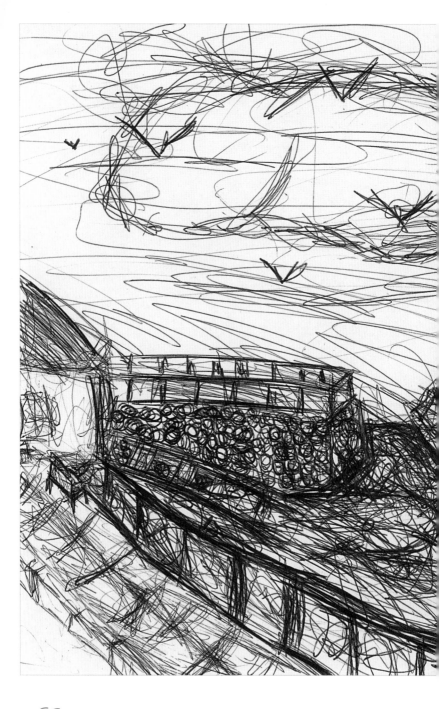

" This is a little beach where I grew up... **"**

>> 298

THIRTEEN SENSES/
TOM WELHAM

Summertime

Spiderman pyjamas

door to the attic

❝ I'd float out of my bed and out of the bedroom door, then down the stairs to the front door... ❞

>> 299

flying

Me asleep

monsters under the bed

Scott Paterson

SONS AND DAUGHTERS/
SCOTT PATERSON
Strange Childhood Dream

❝Behind every bush a little devil is hiding...❞

>> 300

DIE TÜREN/
MAURICE SUMMEN
Fear of the Devil

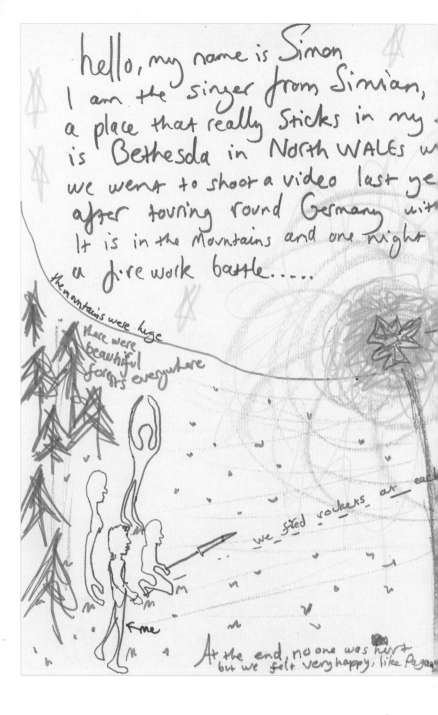

66 It was like being in a gang, doing stupid things together... 99

>> 301

the moon shone very bright

A goat and a squirrel watched

the land was very green

...ap.

...her we had a party, woo!

some people ate friendly shrooms

SIMIAN/
SIMON LORD
Firework Battle

10 <<   On the left is me in my bedroom.
That's where I did most of my
songwriting. I've got my knee
hanging out my bed, because I broke
it when I was playing football. While
I was recovering I was reading books and learning to
play the guitar and writing songs. I still hadn't taken
down all the posters in my room, so there were still some
Stone Roses posters and pictures of Charlie Chaplin and
the big picture from the album <u>The Holy Bible</u> by the
Manic Street Preachers.

This place is the field next to my house. Whenever
anything good or bad happened, I ended up there on that
field, either with my friends or on my own kicking a
football. The wall with all the graffiti on it is where we
hung out. I never got hold of any spray cans, but I drew
little cartoons on the wall with markers. People would
come from all over the place to put graffiti on the wall.
Every few weeks there was something new. It was cool!

The band spent many hours there planning and coming
up with ideas. The guy sitting on the wall is my friend
Steven: we dedicated the album <u>Faded Seaside Glamour</u>
to him, because he was killed in a car crash. The crashed
cars and flames are because the little kids kept stealing
cars and crashing them up in the fields and setting them
on fire... bored kids, you know. Basically I grew up there.

COLDPLAY/
GUY BERRYMAN
The Pompidou Centre, Paris

I was about eight years old when I was walking around with my mother in the Pompidou Centre and got lost. It's obviously a very complicated building. Suddenly I was on the roof,

12 <<

where I wasn't supposed to be. It was very scary, because once the door was shut I couldn't get it open again. So I was stuck on the roof of the Pompidou Centre!

I can just remember the door closing and me being stuck out there. I think somebody had followed me, came up to the roof and brought me down. I can't remember that much about it or what my mother said. I just remember being terrified and feeling very alone, thinking I was going to die up there on the roof.

JEFFREY
LEWIS
Lower East Side

There are memories and places that are deep in my mind, but there is nothing like NYC. I grew up in downtown Manhattan, so that's the universe to me. We always called it

14 <<

the Lower East Side. I take it some call it the East Village now. I have lived there since I was born. There is just nothing like seeing the same streets and buildings you've seen since you first saw anything. The level of familiarity is just so different for me, compared with any other place on earth. I have travelled a lot, but whenever I come back, the streets and the places I know feel like my family. With my family I lived on East 9th Street, then we moved to East 4th Street. Lots of things have changed there, but the sidewalks and fire hydrants are the same. I still like to go there to see my family and my favourite bands, visit comic book stores and record stores, and get pizza.

THE USED/
QUINN ALLMAN
Stealing Bikes

16 <<   When I was a teenager, me and my friends used to steal almost every bike that we could. I don't know how many we took, but there were a lot of them. We didn't sell them, but  used to collect them in a barn. What a crazy idea! And we never got caught by the police. I have no idea what we intended to do with all those bikes... Maybe I thought that we could organize a place to exhibit our bike collection one day!

THE THRILLS/
CONOR DEASY
Attack by a Japanese Fan

The Fuji rock festival is the biggest
festival in Japan. We played a great
show there in front of an amazing
crowd of people in 2003. And what
I'll never forget is that right after
the concert we got attacked by a Japanese fan.
I have no idea why he did it or what he wanted.
It was really scary!

18 <<

FEEDER/
GRANT NICHOLAS
Godzilla

I drew Godzilla for several reasons.
It obviously stands for Japan. But it
also brings back a lot of memories.
I spent a lot of time there with Jon
Lee, our drummer, who died. The last
time we went there with Jon, we were being filmed
by MTV. Our bass player used to live in Tokyo, he's
Japanese. So it was basically a tour of where he used to
live and work. We met some of his friends and it was all
filmed by MTV. When we were doing this trip, we walked
around the streets, trying to find a place to eat Japanese
food. We went to one of the vending machines on the
street, where you put money in and turn it. Something
comes out and you open it up. It's not like in the UK
where you get some crap, a spider or something. In
Japan the toys are much better. I remember that Jon

20 <<

was very excited about getting a toy for his young son. He turned the handle and a big egg came out. Inside was this Godzilla toy. He couldn't stop talking about it and couldn't wait to give it to his son Cameron. At the end of the trip he gave me the Godzilla and asked me to look after it until he could give it to Cameron. But I didn't get a chance to give it to him before we went back... and then I never saw him again.

It's something that's always on my mind. That's why Godzilla is in there. It's not just a Japanese cultural icon. When someone takes his own life, you can't really understand why. It makes you angry and sad, you feel such frustration. So it represents showing the monster side. When we travel, I miss Jon a lot, and when we go to places I went to with Jon, I miss him even more. I find it harder than actually being in London where we probably spent more time together. Every time I go to Japan, I remember the time we spent there together.

FUCK/
KYLE DARIN STATHAM
Ice Cream Shop in Frankfurt

22 <<   Once upon a time there was a chameleon who lived in Frankfurt and who passed on and also simultaneously there was one Don Geffi who discovered God in an ice-cream cone in Bologna and who, upon hearing of the passing of said chameleon, also thought it meet and right to drink the mirto and then passed out and dreamed of the holy church of Castiglione while the bottle dreamed of a pointy boot and the small grave dreamed of being alive.

TRAVIS/
FRAN HEALY
Hill in Glasgow

There's a hill on the south side of
Glasgow, a beautiful place where you
have a marvellous view over the
city. I went there for the first time
when I was twelve years of age. I

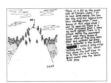

24 <<

was fascinated in a very special way, so that I had to
return to that place many times after. There I have time
to get into myself. This steady place reminds me how
things keep changing in life. I got inspired there, writing
several songs. One of them, which I especially dedicate to
that place, is called 'Walking Down the Hill'. I like to go
there especially in the autumn and winter time when the
leaves have fallen off the trees.

THE CRASH/
TEEMU BRUNILA
Four Finns in Austria

In Finland the landscape is quite flat
and we don't have mountains, except
in Lapland. So when we were on
our first tour abroad, we were
overwhelmed by the mountains and

26 <<

the raw nature of Austria. We were almost trapped in the
mountains because we couldn't find the place where we
had left our car. We wandered away from the car, being
silly, and we thought 'How the hell did we get here?!'
For all we knew, there might have been a shopping mall
just around the corner...

The feeling you get the first time you go abroad, when you fly 2,500 kilometres to somewhere in the middle of the mountains, and there are people with moustaches who sing along to your songs while you play... that was quite a feeling!

IDLEWILD/
RODDY WOOMBLE
House in the Scottish Highlands

28 << Inchnadamph in the Scottish Highlands is a place that for years I drove through because I spent a lot of time in the Highlands. I always quite liked the place but I never  stopped. Just through circumstances we had a friend who had a house up there. When we had a bit of time we moved up to the Highlands for a month, somewhere at the end of nowhere, like a faraway desolate place. That's where we wrote the songs for the album <u>The Remote Part</u>.

AQUALUNG/
MATT HALES
First Piano

I remember an enormous piano in the corner of the room – when I was small, it seemed really big and it was hard to reach up to it. It was kind of mysterious and fabulous. The piano

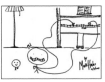

30 <<

was there when I came home from hospital after I was born. My dad was a music lover and he liked the idea that his kid had a piano to play, so he made sure I had one. I think he probably sat me on it in the first few days and I can't ever remember a time when I didn't play.

I played on my own for a few years till I was about eight, then later I took lessons to find out more about the piano, but they were boring. There was always a big difference between how well I could play the piano from sheet music and when I improvised. As soon as I had music in front of me, I couldn't really handle it. So I kept on taking lessons and stopping because I was bored. From when I was really young, teachers – having realized that I was a weird kid – would ask me to write stuff for the school. The first thing I ever performed was a song for the school Christmas concert, when I was about ten years old. My mum still has the programme for that evening with my name on. I used to play little concerts for my grandma and showed her my new songs.

The big-faced person in the picture is me and the little sleepy one is my younger brother Ben. We were always very close. Initially he wasn't as interested in music, but soon enough we started to make music together and we still do today. While music was my big thing, my brother started writing stories and plays. He was going to be the writer and I was going to be the musician. Then we got together, because he would write words for my songs. The hearts in the picture are for the two big things in my life when I was little, the things that I loved more than anything: the piano and my brother.

ADAM
GREEN
My Room

32 <<

This is my old bedroom where I grew up. I lived in that place from when I was four till I was seventeen. It's in a small town called Mount Kisco, which is an hour away from New York. Do I really have to say what was so important about it? It was my bedroom! (laughs). I guess I especially  marked the legs of the chair because they looked like pencils. It's just a memory that I associate with a lot of colour, whereas the rest of my room didn't have that many colours.

It was hard for me to decide if I was going to draw my room like it was when I was about twelve or fourteen. You know, it changed around a little bit. If you look up here, you'll see a bunk bed. I slept on top even though I didn't share the room with anybody. Sometimes if a friend would come over and stay the night, he would sleep in the bottom bunk. I was thought there was a chance that the whole thing could collapse in the night and I would get crushed by the top bunk, so I would always sleep on the top. There was a protective guard rail so that I couldn't fall out, and there was a night light so that I could read books.

Right here is where I had a lot of my recording stuff. I had a four-track-recorder and a CD player and some speakers and some drawing stuff. These were also board games under my bed. Over here is a Meat Puppets poster. I don't know why I had it; they were not such a magnificent band for me! But I liked their second album a lot, and I was in the store and they were selling this poster and I wanted something on my wall, so I picked it. It's funny, when you have the same room from when you're really young and then you grow older, you end up having a lot of junk that you don't really use any more.

HAL/
DAVID ALLEN
Table in the Garden

This is the house of my best friend from school. His parents went away for a month, and me and my friends used to meet up every evening and sit around the table at night time. It was probably the first time that I smoked anything illegal, and it was the first time I heard Bob Dylan  as well. It was something like Bob Dylan's greatest hits, and I kept saying 'Play that tape again, because it's one of the best things I've heard in a long time!' The summer of 1999 was probably the best summer I've ever had! It was great! We used to talk about everything, like life and love and what we would do in the future.

34 <<

MONEYBROTHER/
ANDERS WENDIN
Nobody's Lonely Tonight

The song 'Nobody's Lonely Tonight' is about being out late at night and you look at a girl and think she might be the right one. Then it's like  your life depends on whether you talk to the lady or not, and of course it doesn't, but you've got that feeling... When you're in that state and you feel that emotion, you never give up. You're always looking for somebody. That's the painful side of it. When I wrote that song, I was in that situation almost every night.

36 <<

ART BRUT/
EDDIE ARGOS
Joke Shop

38 <<

In Weymouth there's a road with a joke shop on it and in the summer when I was at my granny's house, I used to go to that shop. It was amazing what you could find there: fake vomit, sweets that would make your tongue hard and things that make your face black – all kind of stupid and

funny things. I didn't buy anything actually, I only used to look!

It was easy to remember which was the right road for the shop, because there was a clock at the end of it. So I used to walk down to the clock and then I could find the way to the shop. I spent every summer at my granny's and before I went home, she always took me to that shop. When I was older, I was allowed to go on my own.

THE CORAL/
JOHN DUFFY
The Zoo

40 <<

When I was a kid I used to live in Manchester. There was a mini zoo in the park and I often went there to watch the foxes and badgers, but I always wanted to go to a proper zoo!

So my dad took me to London Zoo. I remember watching the lions for about two hours. I just stayed there and watched them while they got fed. The next zoo my dad took me to was Chester Zoo. So as a kid I went to the zoo all the time! I loved the snakes and got really sad when I saw the polar bears, they looked as if they were crazy! They've had to stop putting bears in zoos, because their behaviour showed that they didn't feel happy in those circumstances. I've also been to Seaworld in Florida. It was fantastic to watch the big whales! But I haven't been to a proper zoo outside of England. I'm still interested in animals. I've got a dog and a hamster. I used to have two hamsters, but one died. Some day I would love to see a kangaroo or a cheetah for real in the wild!

OCEAN COLOUR SCENE/
STEVE CRADOCK
Scooter Festival, Isle of Wight

The Isle of Wight scooter rally used to happen in the August school holidays. It was a whole weekend, listening to music and dancing, that kind of thing. I used to take part, but not for the last four years. It was probably 1987 that I started going there. I didn't really scooter then... The first scooter I got, when I was twenty-one, got stolen. I've got about six of them now. Five years ago I went back to the Isle of Wight for my honeymoon.

42 <<

INTERPOL/
SAMUEL FOGARINO
A Dream of Philadelphia

This place is from a dream that I had as a child. There was an old newspaper press in a little room that was constructed of wood and very old, maybe from the 18th century.

There was an old woman there who would just stand at the press and constantly print the newspaper. I could never see what was on the newspaper or what it was for. I always tried to look, but I could never focus on what exactly she was printing and what the paper said. But there has never been a point in real life where I felt as safe and as cared for and as loved as I felt by that woman, who didn't even look at me. And I would just sit in the corner of this little room and feel like nothing could ever harm me at all. I never ever wanted to leave!

It became a beautiful thing that I would think about. I still go there in my mind, when I feel really angry or when I think that the world is an awful place and I feel like I have nowhere to go to escape. It's the only place I have that I can go to. It's one thing that I've retained from childhood, probably my best memory. I guess it makes no difference that it was created by my subconscious. Sometimes I feel that the woman in my dream reminds me of the very strong women that I grew up around, like my mother or my grandmother, who were tougher than any men that I have ever met in my life! They were very strong and powerful, physically and mentally. So, I think their influence and inspiration crept into this particular dream. But I think it's just a metaphor for me taking care of myself because I created the whole thing.

CAESARS/
DAVID LINDQUIST
Dead Tree

I've drawn a tree that grew in central
Stockholm close to my home. I used to sit
by the tree when I was a kid. One day,
when I was about seven years old, I came
down to the small park where it stood and
they had cut it down. It broke my heart.
I felt like I had lost a friend.

46 <<

CAESARS/
CÉSAR VIDAL
Sheffield

I don't know anything about
Sheffield, but it's the look of it.
There's a big area with small houses
and they all look exactly the same.
It's kind of depressing and funny at

48 <<

the same time. It makes you wonder what's going on
in the houses. The people go to a factory during the
daytime and come back to their homes at night, and
that's their whole life. I don't really know anything
about the people that live there. It's just an impression...
like a picture in my mind.

DIRTY PRETTY THINGS &
THE COOPER TEMPLE CLAUSE/
DIDZ HAMMOND
House & Family

50 << This is my mum and dad's house, the  place where I grew up, because we are away from home and I haven't been there for a while. All of us in the band are very young, that's why we think of growing up quite a lot, it's a recent memory. I don't want to imagine what my parents say about me being a musician (laughs). It's not the kind of thing you think of as a dream job for your kid, is it? No, I think they are very proud, and obviously they wouldn't really be into that music if their son wasn't in a band. But I think they quite respect the fact that we've done okay out of it and we're able to earn money.

WE ARE SCIENTISTS/
MICHAEL TAPPER
Kittens

52 << A friend of mine took in a stray cat  that used to live outside our practice space. We used to feed it every day and it was really friendly and cute. Then it became wintertime and we thought it would die, so a friend took it in, but his roommate wouldn't let him keep it. So I watched the cat for a couple of weeks and it turned out that the cat was pregnant and had kittens under my bed. Unfortunately

my roommate had a dog, so we couldn't just let the kittens run around the apartment. So they stayed in my room. They were really cute, but also terrors! They refused to use the litter box, so you got little piles of shit everywhere and I was constantly cleaning up. They made a horrible stench in my room. They loved to climb on me when I was sleeping, because they were awake at night, and that was when they wanted to play. Sometimes they just peed on me. After a while I couldn't even sleep in my room, because it was unbearable!

The last time I saw the kittens was when we shot the album cover for <u>With Love and Squalor</u>. We had to give away all the cats right after we started touring, but that period of time just left a mark on my mind. Now I don't know where they are.

LIFE OF AGONY/
ALAN ROBERT
Sad Way Home

Once, when I was in college, I decided to stay home in bed and not go to class. I had a dream that my girlfriend was betraying me. I woke up from the dream and it was so  54 << real that I got myself together and took the bus into the city of Manhattan to confront her. I pulled her out of class and told her I'd had that crazy dream and asked her 'Are you cheating on me?' and she said 'Yeah...'. It was like I'd hit a brick wall and I ended the relationship.

I took the bus home and this shows me in the bus lying with my head against the window, thinking about everything that had happened. That was a big moment for me, because it was one of the first times in my life that a dream became a reality. It's happened several times since then.

FRANZ FERDINAND/
BOB HARDY
My Parents' House

56 <<   This is the house where I stayed from when I was eleven until I was eighteen years old and left home. It's in a suburb of Bradford in the north of England. There it's very  peaceful and just the opposite of Glasgow, where I moved to, which is incredibly busy and lively for music. Bradford was very quiet and dull, but that was good, because you got a lot of time to read and draw and listen to music. I lived there with my parents and my older sister. Actually she moved out when I was quite young, about fifteen. And my parents were never home, because they used to have another house in Scotland where they go – so basically it was my house and I used to be there by myself. So it was great and I had really good parties. I got to be the boss of the house! My parents don't live there anymore; they sold the house and live in Scotland now.

CRISTINA DONÀ

Grandmother's Kitchen

The place that left a trace in my mind is my grandmother's kitchen, where I grew up. I used to go under the table to play with this cat, which wasn't real. It was a statue and I was always afraid that I might break it. It's the place I lived from when I was born until I was ten. The town is called Rho, and is very close to Milan.

58 <<

The problem was that I couldn't go out; the owner of the place didn't want me to go out into the garden. My grandmother died two years ago, she was ninety-nine years old! She was unbelievable, a really beautiful person. At the table I learned to make ravioli and gnocchi. The table was made of marble and wood and was very big – maybe not as big as I've drawn it, but I wanted to give it that feeling. I've drawn the radiator too. in the wintertime my feet were cold all the time so my grandmother used to put the heating on. We also had a TV. It was the beginning of the 70s, so we only had programmes in black and white. So I would watch TV with my feet on the radiator.

THE DRESDEN DOLLS/
AMANDA PALMER
On the Piano

60 <<   The piano I used to play on as a
           child is in my parent's house in a
           suburb of Boston. My mother
           showed me how to play it, so I used
           to sit by myself at the piano in the

living room and try everything out for myself.
I still love doing that today.

When I was older I had piano lessons, but I never enjoyed
them and hated my teacher. I remember that I always
wanted to play music that I'd written myself, which is
what I do now. I was twelve years old when I wrote my
first real song. It was terrible! The music for it is still in
a plastic bag somewhere in the house where my parents
still live.

MUSE/
DOMINIC HOWARD
Baby on Board

62 <<   This is my earliest memory. I was
           one year old, which is extremely
           young, but I can remember vividly
           being on a beach in Spain: I was
           sitting in a white and red rubber

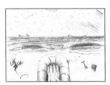

dinghy at the beach, not actually in the water, and could
see it burst in front of me. I was quite upset and started
to cry and get jaded about it.

THE DRESDEN DOLLS/
BRIAN VIGLIONE
My Room When I Was 18

This is a particular evening in my mother's house in New Hampshire where I grew up. I was lying up in the attic, where I would often practise the drums. And this is after

64 <<

I had already moved out and came back one night. I was eighteen years old. I was lying on my back staring up at the light and listening to records on my old stereo, taking in the atmosphere of my childhood things around the attic and thinking of a very good friend of mine, who had killed himself.

There was a bunch of things that my friend had made in one corner, and objects and belongings from my aunt and old posters from when I was thirteen years old. I used to look at these rock stars and think 'God, that's my dream!' I sat next to my drum set and listened to a British punk band. And I just remember this incredible sense of peace and happiness. I felt like I was exactly where I wanted to be at that time, and everything in my life, which had been pretty tumultuous, had just stopped. I said to myself 'I am going to remember this for a long time', enjoying this one solitary moment before moving into the next phase of adulthood.

We have a very old barn that was used in the 1940s and 50s when there were apple orchards behind my house. We turned the back room of it into a clubhouse. All my friends and I used to go there to smoke pot, and talk, and just be together. I remember walking back into that room and getting chills, seeing the kind of makeshift furniture and all the spray paint on the walls, candles that we left there and my dog, who I loved and who just recently was put to sleep. My mom had to bury her in the front yard under a big tree.

STEREOPHONICS/
KELLY JONES
Market Trader

66 << Aberdare Market is where I used to
work and earn some money at the
very beginning of my musical career.
I worked there as a trader at Ernie
and Joyce's market stand. I got a lot

of inspiration from that place! Whenever I had an idea,
I wrote the lyrics down on one of those paper bags so
that I wouldn't forget. A lot of songs from our first
album were written at Aberdare Market.

NADA SURF/
MATTHEW CAWS
Central Park

68 << I've seen the Central Park boathouse
in New York City from two different
perspectives. First in 1978, when I
was a child, I used to go there with
my parents every weekend. It was a

kind of familiar place. Now everything looks different!
The same building has changed into a tourist attraction
and become an expensive restaurant!

JJ72/
MARK GREANEY
Dublin Coast

This beach is about five minutes away from where I live in Dublin, it's called Clontagh. When you walk down the beach, as soon as you have turned around, everything has  70 << changed and it's a completely different place. In most major cities there is no escape from them, but in Dublin you have got this amazing coastline. You can see the city behind it, the chimneys and then the Dublin Mountains. The colours change completely within five minutes. This was actually the first place where I got a song in my head. I was walking back and I could hear the song 'Rosanna' inside my head. I had to go home and write it down. So it's a very important place to me.

The sea is really dirty and polluted, but the sea just takes what it wants with it. I couldn't tell you exactly what goes where, because it changes all the time. When I was young, the sand dunes looked like mountains, they seemed really high. But now they are diminished by wind and water.

The first place I lived in Dublin, the beach was just across the road. The second place, the beach was about ten minutes away. It's some people's favourite place, something like their battery, because everything is constant, everything is the same all the time – it represents security. But beaches fascinate me, every single grain of sand. It's like the beach is a world, and every grain of sand is a person, and they all go into the sea and come back. Our entire second album was actually written with that place in mind.

ATHLETE/
JOEL POTT
Birth of My Daughter

72 <<   I've drawn the hospital where my
first child was born. The place means
a lot to me, because I came there to
see my baby. That little child got
born early and had to spend her first
weeks in an incubator. We were only allowed to see her
at specific times – it seemed quite abnormal because as
parents you want to be with your child all the time and
to take it home. So whenever I came to that room in the
hospital I was really excited! Fortunately everything
went well and we were very happy when we were allowed
to take our daughter home. Our song 'Wires' was written
about that experience.

STARSAILOR/
JAMES WALSH
The Birth

74 <<   Westminster Hospital in Chelsea is
where my daughter Niamh was born
in August 2002. I sat up all night
by the side of the bed where my
girlfriend Lisa was, and went home a
few hours after Niamh was born, at around 5.30 a.m.
The hospital was a normal public hospital so there
weren't any extra beds for partners to stay. I remember
the first time that we put her into the little crib by Lisa's
bed when she was first born; they put the front screen
on the crib and she kept kicking it off. She has been a
lively little child ever since that, really.

I'm away from home a lot and I can't see her that often, but she recognizes my voice on the phone. My girlfriend usually comes out for a few days here and there. She's from Ireland, that's why I've drawn the Irish shamrock there. I'm obviously from England, so it's the two nations joining together. The Liver Bird is because I'm a Liverpool supporter.

2RAUMWOHNUNG/
TOMMI ECKHART
Stereo

Lying in bed listening to music is just the best thing. There's a music system right next to the bed and I've set up two big speakers at the head end. When you lie in the middle of  76 <<
the bed between the speakers, it feels like you aren't just hearing the music with your head, but with your whole body. To really get that feeling, the music needs to have a lot of bass. It feels almost like flying.

I like to lie back on the pillows, listen to the music and smoke dope, but it's good without the dope too. It's an amazing experience that never gets old!

BELLE AND SEBASTIAN/
CHRIS GEDDES
DJ Night in Glasgow

A few years ago I used to do a night
at a club called 'Yang' in Glasgow.
It was the only time I've ever had
my own club night running regularly.
I did it for about a year. It was called
'The Night' after the Frankie Valli song. That's the view
from behind the wheels of steel. It was a mixture of
Northern Soul, funk and disco and on a good night
I would be playing house and techno records by end of
the night. It depended on the crowd, if people were up
for the madness.

The night only ran for a year and in the course of that,
there were maybe half a dozen nights that were really
special. It was on a Tuesday so most of the time it was
quite quiet. It's how I met my current girlfriend. When
I started out doing these nights she was just working at
the bar but during the year that I was doing the club
she became the manager of the place.

It ended in quite sad circumstances for everyone. The
ownership changed and all the DJs and staff either left
or got fired. But on Fiona's big leaving night, the two of
us got together and we have been going out ever since,
so it was a happy ending for us.

OASIS/
NOEL GALLAGHER
Ibiza Smiley

Ibiza is just a great place to hang
out. I have a house there, and I
sometimes go there to get crazy or
to relax... but mostly to get crazy,
I think. I related it to a smiley
because people there are always happy, and this is
the face of the acid house culture of the eighties,
which is associated with Ibiza.

80 <<

The first time I went to Ibiza was 1998–99. An advert
for a house in Ibiza in an English newspaper caught
my attention. So I phoned the people up, and got on
an aeroplane, with the intention of seeing the house,
and I liked it so much that I bought it. You can go to
clubs there until 6 o'clock in the morning and take lots
of fucking drugs. But you can also go there and relax
in some parts, where it's really quiet.

Sometimes I go there with friends and sometimes alone,
it depends. The last time I went alone. You make plenty
of friends there. In addition Ibiza can be a place of
inspiration. I have written a few songs there. I don't
know if any of them are special and I am not sure
whether I have recorded those ones. I have a very bad
memory for that kind of thing. Maybe I should date my
lyrics, but I don't. But I remember writing quite a lot
of songs in Ibiza. Maybe I didn't record a lot of them,
either because they weren't very good, or because I
was too high...

KAISER CHIEFS/
RICKY WILSON
House in Leeds

82 << This is a house that I'm trying to buy at
the moment. It means a lot to me, because
I wasn't able to afford it until we had some
success. I don't really want to buy fast
cars or long expensive holidays. There's
nothing I really want to have but this
place. It's like all our success turned into
stone. It's a real embodiment of everything we've
achieved.

When I saw the house the first time from the outside, I
didn't even have to walk around it. I knew it was the one
and I had to get it! It's in Leeds and it's got four rooms,
which is a lot for one person! But the way I look at it, I
would like to live there forever, so it might not just be for
one person forever. It makes you feel quite grown up to
buy a house or an apartment. You feel like you've lost a
little bit of your youth, but it is very exciting.

I've made up a superstition... it's a bad habit, but I
always do it. It's bad luck to change the colour of a
house's door. So the last time I moved, I took a little bit
of the turquoise paint of the door to a shop and they
mixed the exact colour for me, and I painted the door
again with the same colour. I'll do the same with my
new front door and will keep it red!

KEANE/
RICHARD HUGHES
Battle Abbey

This is supposed to be Battle Abbey in East Sussex, and it was built to commemorate the Battle of Hastings in 1066, when the Normans came and invaded. They beat the English  84 <<
army and William the Conqueror built the abbey to commemorate his victory. I'm afraid the drawing doesn't really do it justice, because it's a beautiful building. I'm also colour-blind so I don't really know which is green and which is brown so I did it in black! I tried to make the picture 3-D, because there are more towers in the background, but it looked so rubbish that I gave up!

On the left you have a little path, and when I go running – that's how I'm trying to keep fit – I run from my house, which is about two miles off to the left, all the way to the abbey, and I go through one of these gates, and I go past this bench. I remember sitting there with Tim after we'd got very drunk one night. I live at one end of the town and Tim lives at the other end, and Tim, whenever he gets drunk, decides he has to go home. So he wanted to go home! We walked home and I remember that we stopped for a rest because we were feeling a bit dizzy, so we sat on that bench. So that's why the bench is there!

SPARTA/
MATT MILLER
Ship

86 <<   When we are on tour we travel a lot
and go to many different places in
the world. It's great! But although I
see new places and meet new people,
it feels like I'm travelling in a kind of

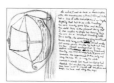

bubble that I never really get out of. It's like travelling
on a ship with familiar people, like the crew and the rest
of the band, and also familiar surroundings.

WE ARE SCIENTISTS/
CHRIS CAIN
Mineshaft Canary

88 <<   This is our tour bus, which we call
the Mineshaft Canary because it's
yellow. Without it, touring is a
waking nightmare. In retrospect I
don't know how we ever did anything
without it! A hotel bed is definitely more comfortable
than the small bunks, but you don't know how soul-
crushing it is to spend each day driving from town to
town. It makes you think that the only thing that you
are accomplishing with your life is 45 minutes of playing
every night. When you do that for month after month
and you feel like only 45 minutes out of every 24 hours
count for anything, you really start to wonder why you
are alive! So the bus drives at night, we get into town by
mid-morning and mostly we waste the day. We can stroll
around and look at the trees or buy coffee at a shop.
They seem like simple pleasures, but in many ways it's
like being released from prison.

ESKOBAR/
ROBERT BIRMING &
FREDERIK ZÄLL
Tour Bus

We just love touring; it's the best
thing to do. The bus takes us to
different places around the world
where we haven't been before. I
think a normal person who had a
look around the bus would ask 'How the hell do you
manage to spend more than an hour in there?!' But we
have a really good time. It's not the most comfortable
way of living, but it's the most fun way.

90 <<

The bus has let us down quite a few times! Even our
driver let us down once. We had an incident a couple
of years ago with a driver who was drinking and driving,
and smoking pot and driving. He was totally crazy and
we didn't get along very well. So our tour manager had
an argument with him and finally he locked us out of the
bus, took the keys and ran away somewhere. All our
instruments and things were inside, so we had to break
into our own tour bus. You really have to enjoy this
whole thing about being on the road and playing music.
If you think you are just going to be a rock'n'roll star
and everything is just stars and glamour, you couldn't
make it through the day. If you're not one hundred
percent dedicated to your music and touring, it can be
really stressful. But for us it's great fun!

KAISER CHIEFS/
NICK HODGSON
Toilet

92 << This is what you need on tour! I've
drawn a toilet and it's very clean!
There's plenty of toilet paper and a
very efficient curtain, so that no one
can see in. There's a sink with two
taps, hot and cold, a soap dispenser, a hand dryer,
a mirror and a good sturdy lock.

In the past when you got out of the bus and you needed
a toilet, it could be a challenge: no seat on the toilet, no
toilet paper, no nothing. And on toilets in buses you can't
poo! We were always looking forward to arriving at the
next good hotel. Fortunately times have changed.

THE CAESARS/
NINO KELLER
Traffic Accident

94 << This story happened about six years
ago on a highway in the middle of
Sweden. I was on tour and was hired
to play the drums. We were
travelling by bus when suddenly our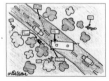
driver had a heart attack and the bus went off the road.
He was lying all over the steering wheel and only at the
last second our tour manager got him away from it and
managed to get us back on track before we hit any other

cars. Later we found out that the driver had had a lot to drink the day before. That's the closest I have been to death or being crippled. I could have been thrown out of the front window. When I think of that moment I still feel scared and uncomfortable and I can still feel the shock!

FUCK/
GEOFFREY HAROLD SOUL
Small Town Magic Show

We had some free time before a show, and on a walk around the town I came upon a theatre where a local magic show was about to begin. It was a mix of local amateurs and a few regional professionals. I was impressed by the attempts of all the performers, from the eleven-year-old

96 <<

beginner to the professionals, to create an effect with their magic-related skills.

THE HIVES/
CHRIS DANGEROUS
From the Drummer's Point of View

98 <<   I drew the place where I sit for more
than an hour every night. That's the
view from behind my drums looking
at Nicholaus, Pelle, Matt and Carl,
and at a lot of people with happy
faces. It's something that I'll remember forever, because
I do it a lot. It's not a specific place, but it is in some
ways, because we create the place every night. So it
could be pretty much anywhere. It's the place I like
most, probably. I wish I could be down there in the
crowd, looking at the five of us at the same time. We try
to play every night. We don't like days off. And even if
we've played a show already, we might try to do a second
gig in a smaller club. That feeling and the feeling when
you've made a good record are probably the best feelings
you can have.

OCEANSIZE/
MIKE VENNART
Stoned at Glastonbury, Watching Travis

100 <<   The Glastonbury Festival is probably
the best festival in the world! Not
that I've been to all the festivals in
the world, but I've been to a lot and
to every other festival in Britain.
Just the general atmosphere of the place makes you
enthusiastic and really optimistic about absolutely
everything. Sometimes there aren't any good bands

playing but you still go because of the atmosphere. It's so uplifting! Festivals are quite often about seeing bands, but Glastonbury is a lot more than that. It's been going since the seventies so it's got a real heritage and all the hippies and wizards. It's a very special place, I think.

I was there with my girlfriend Beth in 2000: we had only been going out for about three weeks. And we watched Travis against my will. She's quite a fan and I'm not – it's really not my kind of music. But I ended up so absolutely happy and beside myself with joy that I thought that Travis were in fact the greatest band in the world... It was just one of those moments – me and my girlfriend were really loved up and admitted to each other that we were really in love, and we'd never said that to each other before. So Travis was a soundtrack to that kind of bonding, which is a shame. I wished it could have been something cooler and a lot more meaningful to ME, but unfortunately it was Travis! But they were really good that night!

COSMIC CASINO/
MESS
Bohemian Rhapsody

We were on a week-long tour with the Scottish band Aereogramme, and after a gig at the Schlachthof in Wiesbaden, we all sang 'Bohemian Rhapsody' together. We hadn't known

102 <<

each other previously, and the Scots are just as reserved as we Bavarians are, so it took us a while to get to know each other.

But after the Wiesbaden gig we were all friends. Also, by that point, nobody could remember how much we'd all had to drink. That's when we all sang the Queen song.

CLIENT/
CLIENT B
Backstage in Cologne

104 <<   This happened when we were playing a support show for Erasure in Cologne. When we were looking for our cloakroom, we couldn't find it. Then someone came up to us and 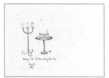 showed us where we could dress up. It was really amazing. They'd built us a small place behind the stage surrounded by amplifiers and carriage boxes. The whole place looked just like I drew it. There was just a small table, but there was a big candlestick too which made the whole situation more impressive. When you are on tour it often feels like a neverending story but on days like this there are still some surprises left.

THE VON BONDIES/
JASON STOLLSTEIMER
Polaroid

We were in New York playing the Mercury
Lounge about three years ago, and this
guy in his thirties came up to me and said
'You know, you really helped me through
some troubled times.' And he showed me
this photo of his sister from the prom.
That was the last time he ever took a

106 <<

picture of her. She had killed herself. He said a song that
I had written called 'Nite Train' had really helped him.
He took the lyrics upon himself and came out with his
own meaning.

Our songs are serious, not just jokey rock'n'roll songs,
and that was the first time I really realized that they
could touch someone. This is a picture of his sister that
he gave me, which was really sad, because she looks so
happy, like a prom girl. He gave me the picture and he
said 'Thanks!' to me. Then he left and didn't stay for the
show. I still think about it all the time.

BLOC PARTY/
GORDON MOAKES
Backstage Idyll

Hammocks and trees make me think
of a festival in America that we
played with The Pixies. The venue
had a whole garden behind the stage.
You could just go and lie there in a

108 <<

hammock, and you could walk in the woods. It was
really peaceful!

I remember that day was really humid. We had finished our tour through America where we had spent most of the month. After all the days of hard work we had a peaceful afternoon, just lying in hammocks, drinking beer – although no one was supposed to be drinking! – and it just felt really nice. We have played some really nice tours but you don't often get a chance to sit and relax.

MANDO DIAO/
GUSTAF NORÉN
Shed

110 << This is our first rehearsal place. We spend a whole summer there, writing new songs. We didn't have a key so we had to break the window and climb in. Then I would go to the  back and open the door for Björn to get in. The community owned the building, but it was closed in the summer so we could use it. They always used to put in a new window so that we could smash it again and go in with our instruments. And on the upper level we played pool. It was kind of the leisure level, where we used to play video games and have big parties. On the lower level we rehearsed. This is where the audience stood when we played live. We invited our friends and put the drums there and the guitars.

The word 'torpet' is Swedish and means a small house, like a summer house. The house still exists. Even Jimi Hendrix has been there. He was supposed to go to Stockholm, but his plane had problems and had to land in our town. The airport is close by and he came here.

TELE/
MARTIN BROMBACHER
Rehearsal Room

This is our new rehearsal room; as I'm drawing this picture, it's still being renovated. This is where we spend most time together – when we don't have anywhere else to go, that is.

112 <<

LOUIS XIV/
JASON HILL
Recording Studio

My recording studio is my favourite place in the world to be, it's sort of my little playground. I've always had one since I was eleven years old. It started with a little one-track cassette recorder and my bedroom was my recording studio. Then I went to a four-track and an eight-track and then a sixteen-track. The room got bigger and bigger and just became my playground with all the instruments. It's where my mind is all the time.

114 <<

The recording studio is in San Diego in an old church. It's a store-front Baptist church that had a congregation of forty people. The moment they moved out, we grabbed it. It's got big ceilings and old tiles. It looks like Motown or Abbey Road in 1964 in a weird way.

A couple of months ago I was homeless. Usually I would just sleep at a girlfriend's house at four in the morning.

That was all right, but I didn't have a proper place to live. For years I just slept on the floor of the studio, bundling a bunch of clothes together to use as a pillow. But some time ago I bought a house for myself and spent a fortune on a nice big bed. So now it's kind of hard to get out of bed in the morning.

THE SHINS/
MARTY CRANDALL
Rehearsal Room

116 <<

This is our rehearsal room, where the band formed. We used to spend a lot of time there, and a couple of strange and funny things happened. The bathroom was downstairs, and since the house was so old, there were tree roots growing into the plumbing. The toilet and the shower overflowed with water and completely covered the whole basement with a layer of horrible sewage!

But the good thing was that some of our not so important instruments were down there and the insurance money meant we could get brand new equipment and a new carpet, and paint the walls. So in the end it was even better for us! Something that could have been horrible was actually a blessing in disguise.

HOOBASTANK/
MARKKA LAPPALAINEN
Bob the Bass Tech

Being on stage is my job. This is a picture of my bass tech, Bob; we call him Bobba! It's a portrait of Bobba and his bass teching skills. We've known each other for about a year. It's kind of an intimate relationship, all sweaty and disgusting (laughs). We hang out, drink a little bit,  118 << talk about the show – he's my buddy! He used to be Papa Roach's bass tech, but we needed a bass tech, so our tour manager stole him from Papa Roach.

We do about 300 shows a year and that's where we live, on stage! We all bought a house in Los Angeles from our success. What sucks is that we never get to see the house; it's more like a storage room. But this is what we do; it's a lot of fun and it's a lot of work.

THE KILLERS/
RONNIE VANNUCCI JR
Garage

This is my parents' garage in Las Vegas, where I used to live. It's a place where I used to spend a lot of time as a kid. While the other kids were riding mountain bikes, I'd be  120 << inside the garage singing and beating on the washer, dryer and refrigerator. One Christmas, I think I was eleven, they all broke down and my Mum bought me a drum set! That was the start of something beautiful. When I got the drums, I got right on and didn't really have a problem working with them but I wanted to get some formal lessons. It started there and I ended up majoring in music with percussion performance at college and learning that way. Before The Killers I played in different bands – arty bands and also jazz combos and orchestras.

SUGARPLUM FAIRY/
CARL NORÉN
First Gig

122 << This is our first gig together. Victor used to play the bass all the time but one day we released him to the microphone so he could rock. It was a special day that day. There were  some record companies in the audience and afterwards we got signed. All our lives have revolved around the band for the last eight years, that's why life in the band is almost our only memory.

THE DATSUNS/
DOLF DE BORST &
PHIL BUSCHKE
Tour Impressions

We grew up in Cambridge, New Zealand, and we wanted to tour the world, which is what we're doing now. This picture is about some funny things that have happened on tour. Not everything could fit on the page. At the top I've drawn the bus that we are sitting in. The guy who is looking at us is Ian, the bus driver, who's asleep. The wheels are apples, because we get lots of apples on the tour. There are bits of fruit just everywhere. The cloud and lightning are taken from the cover of the Hellacopters' album <u>By the Grace of God</u>, but I kind of made it into the smoking wheels from the bus.

124 <<

We play every night and a lot of times we play with the Gaza Strippers. So we all share everything and we are all like a big family. At the London show all of the Hellacopters got up and played a song with us.

The dice stands for a game that the Hellacopters showed us. You have to roll the dice and try to get to 100. If you roll a one then you go back to zero. But if you keep rolling the dice and you get to, let's say, 41, you can choose to stop and pass the dice on to the next person. And then the next time it's your turn, you can keep going and you might get up to 70. But if you roll a one, you have to go back to 41. We played that game a lot and we bet money on it so that's why the Euro is there.

We bought a four-track recorder because we've been on tour for so long and we need to write new songs and record on the bus. Well, our four-track got stolen and we had to buy another one. So the hand and the '4' is the scum stealing our four-track. The glass of wine is because a lot of red wine has been drunk on the tour.

Tonight we were recording a song and we recorded the bass track in the bunker, which is under the Batschkapp in Frankfurt, where we just played. It was just a bass and drum track for the b-side of our next single that's coming out, but we got told off for doing it. As soon as we had finished recording the tracks, someone busted in and asked 'What're ye doin' in here?!' and we were like 'Uhhh!' and had to get out. It was lucky we got it down in time.

'Let's do it' is like an in-joke for us. We didn't realize it, but every time we play, in between songs we say 'Let's do, let's do it!' and the Hellacopters picked up on it and so did the Gaza Strippers.

STARS/
GROUP COLLAGE
Tour Images

126 << The picture is a kind of group collage by all the members of the band. Everyone tried to express and represent some of the feelings we have when we are on tour. We just  wanted to give some impressions and want to leave them without any more comments.

DEATH CAB FOR CUTIE/
NICHOLAS HARMER
My View

We played a show in Los Angeles
and had to leave right after to head
for the next venue. So I got on the
bus at night time, with all the
impressions of Los Angeles in my
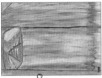
head: Technicolor lights, crowds of people, buildings
everywhere. With that picture in my mind, I fell asleep
in the bus. And the next morning I woke up but when
I looked out of the window I saw a completely different
landscape. Green as far as the eye could see! I was
really flashed! It really gave me the feeling of being
on the road and travelling around.

128 <<

SPEARMINT/
JAMES PARSONS
Inside the Tour Bus

When you asked us to represent a
place we have a real fondness for, I
was unsure of how to narrow it down
to just one location. So our idea was
to draw our vehicle that transports

us from A to B. The image was created on the move in
the tour bus as we hurtled down the Autobahn with
whatever art materials you gave us. You'll notice that
the only person talking is the driver.

130 <<

DEATH CAB FOR CUTIE/
CHRIS WALLA
Hotel

132 <<   The place that left a trace in my
          mind is the atmosphere I find when
          I enter into a new, fresh hotel room.
          It doesn't matter where it is. When
          we are on tour we get to see a lot of
          different hotel rooms, but they all have
          a similar atmosphere.

THE LIBERTINES &
BABYSHAMBLES/
PETE DOHERTY
Moscow

134 <<   Moscow always existed in my
          imagination. When I was living on
          the dole in London and didn't have
          any money, I was quite a poet. Some
          people got some money together

from the Arts Council and they sent some unemployed
kids and some artists over to Moscow, so I went to do
poems in Russia. I didn't know what to expect. Every
night we did a show and it was always chaos.

A filmmaker took me out to the slums of Moscow. I
remember I spent four days there. They didn't speak any
English and I didn't speak any Russian. They were really
poor. They used to spend time out in these dark forests,
which I have drawn. All kinds of weird things were going
on there... strange little kids with big heads would kill

animals and butchers chased them. And we made a little film, it was a bit dark actually, and in the film I had to pretend that I raped a girl, who was an actress. Yeah, it was strange, but I fell in love with her anyway. I lived with her for four days. And when I wanted to go back to Moscow, she turned out to be insane – she wouldn't let me go. When I was asleep she tied me up and I woke up locked in the room. I managed to get free, but I couldn't get out of that place. It was in the middle of the night. But somehow I made it back to Moscow and that's when I discovered the weird, fucked-up underworld of Moscow, the Mafia drug ghettos, it was great. I was in a Russian ecstasy.

I was only there for about two weeks, but in that time it was just so weird, NOT speaking any Russian, NOT having any money, but performing every night. It was just complete freedom. Not knowing where I was going to stay or what I was going to do… just with my guitar on my back and a long cape. The whole thing was about trying to survive. There were no boundaries, anything was possible and could have happened and did happen. Yeah, it's just a very romantic time in my head, but dangerous too – just cool!

BLACK REBEL MOTORCYCLE CLUB/
NICK JAGO
Image of the Festhalle

The place that left a trace in my mind is the Festhalle in Frankfurt. It was used for gathering Jews before they had to go to the concentration camp. Yeah, this building, we found that out. But you could tell that the building had some

136 <<

kind of Nazi connection, because as soon as you look up to the roof it looks like that really dramatic Nazi architecture. That's where this image came from. When you look up you can see the black railings and stuff with the Nazi symbol on. It makes you think of blood and killings and stuff.

THE (INTERNATIONAL) NOISE CONSPIRACY/
DENNIS LYXZÉN
Protest in Gothenburg

138 <<   In 2001 there was a huge protest against the European Union summit and George W. Bush in Avenyn, the main street in Gothenburg. About 20,000 people turned up and there were crazy riots for two days. We went there to protest and then we played a show for all the protesters the  day after. Me and the other guys got stuck in the middle of the riots. It was insane! I always think about it when I come back to Gothenburg. You saw windows getting smashed, kids getting beaten up, and policemen shooting people down. They shot three people, and they don't use rubber bullets in Sweden. They use live ammunition. The cops came from the sides and attacked people with dogs, and people started throwing rocks at the cops. Then they started fighting, all down the main avenue, and smashed up all the stores. For about four hours the protesters attacked and the cops ran back, and then the cops attacked and the protesters ran back. Back and forwards and back. After four hours it dissolved because people kind of ran the wrong way. Later that night there was

another big riot and we saw a kid, about 22 years old, get shot by the police and he almost died. He was in a coma for a month. We were recording <u>A New Morning</u> at the time, and when we went back to the studio after everything that had happened, it felt like we had a lot more to say. You know, we talk about politics and we sing about politics all the time but that was the first time we actually saw class struggle in real life.

SPARTA/
TONY HAJJAR
Last Days in Lebanon

Beirut in Lebanon is where I was born. In December 1979, when I was five years old, we flew to the US. When we left there was a civil war going on, and my last memory of the  140 << night before we left is a missile stuck in the top of our apartment building that didn't go off. So that could have been my last night, but for some reason it didn't explode. I remember walking on top of the building and seeing it!

The next day we got our flight to El Paso in Texas, to live there. For some reason a lot of my relatives who moved to the US moved to that city. There we lived in a red house and that's where I started playing drums. My mother was sick and that was my way of dealing with things. I spent most of the time growing up with her in hospital, and I've included the date that she passed away. That's how I remember my young life. I lived in El Paso until 1999, when I moved to Los Angeles. I haven't been back, but I definitely want to.

LIFE OF AGONY/
KEITH CAPUTO
September 11

142 <<   I was on the roof of my apartment in
Brooklyn and I was overwhelmed by
what I was looking at, because from
my roof you could see the Twin
Towers. I have been all over the

world, and I've sat in open fields and tasted eternity, but
this was a different eternity. That place left serious
imprints on the world's heart and on my own.

What is interesting is that when I was a child I had a
recurring nightmare of soldiers standing stiff and
uptight and I would see buildings crashing down. This
little image would get so huge in my mind that my uncle
used to find me underneath the living room table and
wake me up, and I would be kicking and screaming and
wouldn't know how I'd actually got underneath the table.
I remember getting really sick as a child with the flu, my
throat closed up and I kept having that nightmare of the
city crumbling. When this happened, it was the first place
that my mind and heart brought me to. That place has
brought me to places of extreme peace and joy that I
have never experienced before...

SNOW PATROL/
NATHAN CONNOLLY
I Love NY

New York is a place I've always wanted to go, ever since I was a child. I don't know why I have a fascination with it, a romance. But you know, when you grow up all

144 <<

these images from films obviously stick in your mind. Everywhere you go in the world, you get to see images of New York.

The first impression of New York was exactly what I had imagined. It's just incredible. You stand there and can see nothing but streets. We went to a café on a corner and it was just so New York. People were sitting there eating their meat sandwiches and drinking Dr. Brown's root beer, and I was just listening to the people talking. It couldn't have been more New York, all the pictures on the wall and all the people. It's just a great city. I could even imagine moving to New York. Who knows, maybe if I earned a lot of money, because I would need to! I want to go back and spend more time there.

I AM KLOOT/
JOHN BRAMWELL
First Time in Berlin

I find Berlin exotic in a very austere way. Obviously historically it's an incredible place. You can't really imagine what it must have been like in Germany during the Second World

146 <<

War and the Cold War, to see the buildings that the Nazis built and then to see the buildings that the Russians built. It's all about these monoliths and this imposing stuff and yet there's tremendous freedom artistically. I find it a terrific, exciting place. Not that it's a beautiful city to look at – it isn't! It's very spooky. Obviously lots of people from the music industry have spent time there: Brian Eno, David Bowie, Lou Reed, Nick Cave and PJ Harvey, all people I have a lot of respect for.

The first time I saw Berlin about three years ago, it was a very stormy day and I was on the west side of the wall. And I could imagine the Russians, ten years previously, all saying 'We are here! We are here!' (imitates a Russian accent). When we play abroad, it's the town that feels most like Manchester. The first time we played there it was for a hundred people and when we played there about two months ago it was for about eight hundred people. I think they got us kind of quickly.

CLIENT/
CLIENT A
Russian Badge

148 << I have been obsessed with Russia since I was a child. Dostoevsky is my favourite author and I read <u>Crime and Punishment</u> under the bedcovers. I was sixteen years old when I joined the Socialist Party and thought I would change  the world. I went to university and studied Russian history, and fell in love with the Bolsheviks and Lenin. I guess I first went to Russia expecting something of that, but it was so different. The band have been there about

five times now. If we are offered a Russian gig once or twice a year, we always say yes – we love going there. It's totally on the edge, like another world. St Petersburg and Moscow are the most interesting places to go. Moscow is almost like the Russian New York.

THE WEDDING PRESENT/
DAVID GEDGE
London Bridge in Lake Havasu

At the end of our last North American tour, my girlfriend and I drove from New York to Seattle via Los Angeles, and we did a lot of sightseeing on the way. Everyone

150 <<

said 'Whatever you do, you must go and see the Grand Canyon,' so we did, but I have to say that I was actually a bit disappointed. You're led to believe that it's going to be the most impressive thing on earth, but it's just a big valley, really. I think the Alps are just as good, and there are also places in Scotland that are as beautiful. But afterwards we drove to Lake Havasu in Arizona. It was extremely hot there: it was 40º C at 9 p.m.! But I'd heard the story about the London Bridge that's been rebuilt in the middle of the desert, so I was interested to see it for myself. It's a fascinating concept.

There have been about five London Bridges over the River Thames. I think the first couple were wooden and then they started building stone versions. In the sixties they realized that the current bridge was no longer strong enough for the heavy traffic, so they decided to rebuild it yet again. The city of London basically asked if there was anyone who wanted to buy the old bridge, and

Robert McCulloch, an American entrepreneur from Lake Havasu, thought that he could transform the town into a popular tourist resort by using the bridge as an attraction. So he bought it for $2,460,000 and the agreed price was, interestingly, based in part on his own age. I guess he was pretty eccentric. In 1968 they dismantled the bridge, stone by stone. Incredibly, they marked exactly where each and every brick was taken from, shipped it all the way over to America... and then rebuilt it!

It's very odd, because the surrounding area is just like typical American desert, you know – palm trees, gas stations, motels, a shopping mall, half-naked teenagers on boats... and then, right in the middle, there is this completely inappropriate-looking huge old bridge made from stone. I found that more impressive than the Grand Canyon! I just find it fascinating that someone decided to pursue such a strange and ambitious project.

KEN
STRINGFELLOW
Faroe Islands

152 << The Faroe Islands are somewhere between Iceland and Norway in the North Atlantic. They have a distinct culture and language there, which is quite similar to Icelandic. Not a lot of  people live there, maybe between 40,000 and 50,000. The islands have a look that can't be captured here; they look like they were just raised out of the sea yesterday. Most of them are so steep and there's water running off

the sides. There's a sort of <u>Lord of the Rings</u> look to the place, it's kind of lonely.

I went there with a punk band called White Flag and we played two shows there. They were the craziest shows I have ever played. People there start working when they are really young. They basically need everybody to work and most of the work is fishing. So they have their fun and sow their wild oats when they're thirteen. When we played there, the crowd was mostly kids and they were grinding against each other and it was just very sexual. The girls were licking my hands while I played – it was really insane! They go really wild for a couple of years and then they get married and work. Fishing is not just men's work; the girls have to do it as well. It's a marvellous place. The way they are is so isolated. It's also one of the cleanest places in the world. A real oasis.

MELISSA
AUF DER MAUR
Dream Desert

I had a dream in 1991 that affected my real life so profoundly that it shifted the course of my whole life. So it's one of the most important places I have ever been.

154 <<

The place is a desert, and in the dream a gift was given to the human beings of the planet Earth. A force from up above, whether it was aliens or God or the universe, whatever it was, gave the gift of music. And in this particular place it was the next level of music. They created a pyramid in the middle of nowhere, because it was a three-dimensional sound and that sound was too big to have in a city so they put it out in the middle of the desert in a special structure. A bunch of random people were chosen and brought to that place to experience the first level of the gift, the three-dimensional sound. The people didn't really know what it was, it was just the power of sound. Then they were told to walk along a path, but they didn't know what to do after they had received the gift. So the people just followed the path and then came to a building and they stopped and didn't know what their challenge was. Then it rained and the doors of the building started to close around them. And right at that moment, when they all were about to die in that evil-looking science-fiction building, they realized that only one person needed to make it out of the building to pass on the gift. Then they came together in a group effort and climbed on each other's shoulders. This basically made the people understand that they were all one and that it's not about selfishness, it's about coming together as one unit.

I woke up that morning understanding that music had the power to bring people together, almost like spiritual love or religion. Music was the power that would be able to remind people that if there was a group effort, people could unite and fight against any challenge. And the challenge was sent by the same source that sent the gift, as if to say 'Do you know what to do with this?' All they needed was to get just one person out to tell the rest of the world about the beautiful gift that had been offered to us.

I want to pass on this idea, even if it's just a dream. Passing on the idea of something can give your life direction and bring you to the right place at the right time; it can give meaning to your life. I have never really tried to draw this dream before or even write it down. I just lived it instead. But I can honestly say that this is one of the most important places that I have ever been!

MUSE/
MATTHEW BELLAMY
Psychology Test

This is an imaginary place from a psychological test that my girlfriend, who's a psychologist, showed me. You ask someone to visualize a desert, a cube, some stairs, a glass and a horse. The idea is that the person builds up a mental picture. Afterwards the psychologist can describe what's wrong or what's right with that person.

156 <<

The desert is your perception of the world, and the cube is your perception of yourself. Some people draw a cube of metal or glass; some do a massive one and others a really small one. Stairs represent your friendships. What they are made of, metal or wood, reflects how solid you think your friends are. Also, if the stairs are away from the cube, then you think your friends are far away from yourself. The glass represents love. If there's no liquid inside it, that person needs love. Also, if the glass is inside the cube, it means you have a good relationship with someone. If it's outside the cube, it means that maybe the relationship is finished.

The horse represents the desire for life or desire in general. If it's a white horse then it means innocence. A black horse is a lot less innocent! If the horse is running and very lively, you can say the person is passionate. If one of its legs is broken, maybe the person has a problem with erections. It's a real test that a lot of psychologists do to people! The picture I drew is the same one I drew for my girlfriend, and afterwards she told me what it meant. Basically from now on, I always have that image of the desert in my mind, and the elements in it change depending on how I'm feeling.

MAXÏMO PARK/
PAUL SMITH
Cologne Car Park

158 <<   This is a sort of car park area in
Cologne, which had lots of nice
shapes and colours and a turquoise
tint to the paintwork. It left a strong
imprint on my mind, that's why I

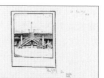

took some photographs and I thought that rather than
invent something, I'd try and use my hand to interpret
it. I just had a nice day, walked around and explored the
city and found out a little bit more about myself and the
place. I thought the area had a character of its own.
Obviously it's anonymous, but it felt like I had something
in common with it. It was desolate but I like the
emptiness of it. It was just a nice space.

MAXÏMO PARK/
DUNCAN LLOYD
Cityscape (NYC)

160 <<   I've been drawing cityscapes ever
since I went to New York for the first
time in 1999. The buildings in New
York left an impression on me and I
started creating cityscapes in my

head from buildings that I had seen. The drawings aren't
actually real streets, but made-up cities. I suppose I'm
quite a visual person so the first thing I do when I come
to a city is to look at buildings, shapes, people and the
whole atmosphere of it. You get a feel for the place when
you look around and walk around. What hits me is what I
see around me.

I used to earn some money in call centres, doing really boring jobs, and I used to draw during work. So I did lots of these drawings and gave them away. Only my favourites I've kept. But I've got lots of paintings at home and a brand new one of Newcastle that I've done. I've also done a really detailed one of Hong Kong, but I've given that away too.

SLUT/
CHRIS NEUBURGER
The Great Stupa

There are a few places on the earth that are sacred, not in a religious sense, but which give you a sense that everything is perfect when you are walking around them. The Great Stupa of Bodnath, a Buddhist monument north-east of Kathmandu, is one such place. You only have to look at it for five minutes to be completely overwhelmed by it. I was there in 1995 and I've never forgotten it. I went to Nepal while I was studying architecture. It was the first time I'd ever gone on a trip like that with a friend.

162 <<

PHOENIX/
LAURENT BRANCOWITZ
Tokyo

164 <<   I went to Tokyo a couple of weeks ago and it was a mysterious revelation. The city has a lot of power. It's like a body where you can see the blood pulsating. You can feel

when you are in tune with the rhythm with the city, which was not difficult. It was hard to admit that it was perfectly the right rhythm.

...TRAIL OF DEAD/
CONRAD KEELY
Valeovlers

166 <<   When I was about fourteen I started to work on a fantasy novel which one day I hope to complete. It's set in a place called Valeovlers.

It's a place on this massive planet where technology had been destroyed. Several thousands of years passed and the planet went back to the Dark Ages. Then some archives were found and the people were able to rediscover their former technology, so once again they were reintroduced to the space age and the rest of the galaxy. The galactic civilization had continued to move on, but the reintroduction was so fast that the culture still remained very medieval in style. It's a planet where there would be computers and spaceships but at the same time people would still ride horses and use swords. Even though they were part of the space age, they would live in a medieval culture.

I'm still working on that novel. In fact I've got the book with me that I do all my notes in (takes out a sketchbook with lots of drawings and notes). These are some of the people that populate that place in the novel. There is a part that takes place in a castle.... where is it? (Turns to a page with a detailed map and drawing of a castle.) I used a postcard of a castle as the basis for the design of my fantasy castle. Right now I'm working on a topographic sketch of the castle and the family tree. It's really complicated! I've been working on it for about fifteen years and I don't know how the story will end.

THE DETROIT COBRAS/
RACHEL NAGY
Black Forest

I lived in Australia for a couple of years with my family because my father used to work for a foreign motor company. They sent me to private school there. We weren't

168 <<

very rich, but at school all the kids had money and horses. So I remember that we used to go to a friend's farm and go horse riding.

A group of us once went horse riding in a black forest with little trees. Suddenly something happened, I don't know whether it was dogs or some wild animals, and the horses went crazy. They started running at breakneck speed between the trees. My horse was trying to knock me off. It was like playing dodgems through the tiny little trees, and we all got banged and bashed while we were trying to guide the horses. It was almost like a video game, only in real life with real danger. It was incredibly terrifying, but really exciting too. It was the most amazing natural adrenalin rush ever. Making it out of there without any help was pretty cool.

The last time I sat on a horse is about a year ago. So when our tour manager asked 'Do you guys have any special requests?', I said 'Yes, I want a pony!' I love riding! One day I'll wake up on a Christmas morning and there'll be a pony under the tree waiting for me. I'll keep on asking and one day someone might give it to me!

THE SOUNDTRACK OF OUR LIVES/
EBBOT LUNDBERG
A Dream About Ghosts

170 <<   This is a dream that I had as a child. I am not really sure if it was a dream or reality, but it's about somebody using an air pump and blowing up ghosts. The faces look like ghosts, but they are balloons at the same time. A very psychedelic dream! It happened so often that I used to joke  about it. But I wasn't sure whether it was aliens or it was a dream. I can't really tell.

I have tried to analyse the dream. I think it has something to do with the idea of pumping up an air bed. It was such an odd dream. It wasn't scary, it was just weird. I wasn't afraid. Maybe I'll put the dream into a song...

KASABIAN/
CHRIS KARLOFF
Clingfilm Cocoon

I won't say much about my work of art. It is just a simple drawing about something happening in a guest house in Bristol in 2001. I call this picture Clingfilm Cocoon. Just make up your own interpretation!

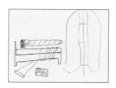

172 <<

BRITISH SEA POWER/
YAN
Pissing in the Stream

This is a simple and joyful work, featuring, on the right, Portly Pisscock. He is a bold young man who gets a lot of pleasure from pissing in a stream. Portly has appeared around the world now and last made a public appearance when British Sea Power played in Japan. Let's hope his piss is healthy.

174 <<

THE RACONTEURS/
BRENDAN BENSON
Amsterdam

176 << Amsterdam never ceases to astound
me. I've been to the Van Gogh
Museum and I've seen the Anne
Frank House, but what really stayed
in my head is the red light district –

it's just such an odd place. When you come from America,
a red light district just feels so bizarre. The first time I
went there was with my girlfriend and she had to leave
immediately after five minutes.

DEATH CAB FOR CUTIE/
NICHOLAS HARMER
Baltimore

178 << (While the other band members
are still busy with their drawings,
he feels inspired and begins a
second artwork.) This is Baltimore!
(laughs and everyone from the band
joins in.)

THIRTEEN SENSES/
ADAM WILSON
John Lennon Memorial Wall

Prague is an amazing place! I went there on holiday after getting engaged. There are couple of places in Prague that are impressive, like the castle and the wall that was a  tribute for when John Lennon died. Everyone who visits the wall signs it.

180 <<

MANIC STREET PREACHERS/
NICKY WIRE
St David's Wood

St David's Wood, place of mystery, purity and joy, now destroyed in the name of progress.

182 <<

SNOW PATROL/
MARC McCLELLAND
Aquarium under the Bridge

184 <<   North Queensferry is about twenty
minutes away from Edinburgh.
Underneath the famous Forth Rail
Bridge is an aquarium called Deep
Sea World. You can wander through
underwater tunnels and see sharks, octopuses and
tropical fish. You get on a conveyor belt and it moves you
along the tunnels as you just stand there. I took my
girlfriend's little sister and brother, three and four years
old, and we had a beautiful day. The kids saw a massive
bridge and they saw sharks and nothing else mattered
the whole day!

EMBRACE/
RICHARD McNAMARA
Lake Constance

186 <<   Sometimes when you're on tour,
you actually get a day off, and if
everyone is in the mood for it, you go
out and have the best day that you
could possibly have. The five of us all
went out to Lake Constance and got a powerboat and just
dived into the lake and swam around all day. It was like
maximum enjoyment! Then the crew posted the pictures
on our website and our partners saw them. So when we
rang that night to say 'Oh, we had a really hard day',
they all said 'But we saw you out at the lake today! You
never worked a day in your lives!' So we got reprimanded
a bit, but at least we had that day of freedom.

2RAUMWOHNUNG/
INGA HUMPE
Copenhagen Airport

188 <<

In December 2004 I wrote the saddest song I've ever written, 'Verlaufen' ('Lost'). I was at Copenhagen airport, intending to go on holiday, but my flight was cancelled. I started to cry, because I'd been waiting for ten hours, but fortunately I had my guitar with me. When I feel really down and things are going badly, something beautiful always comes out of it. In this case, it was this song.

The drawing features things that are mentioned in the lyrics: 'Can't see a window, a door, a light / I don't know myself', and 'I'm a zombie, a ghost / and everything that is sick.' And the song asks the rather metaphysical question: does love exist, or doesn't it?

JOHNNY
MARR
Arizona Desert

190 <<

This is the Arizona desert near the Catalina Mountains. I've been there a few times. I like to go there to make myself feel small and to get really quiet. You can find out some pretty useful and interesting things about yourself and about your world. It's better for me than sitting in the suburbs taking drugs, which is what I used to do before. It's good for the soul.

I first went there 1997. My wife went there first and she came back and was kind of tripped out. I saw the effect it had on her. So I promised myself I would get out there, so we went together and after that I went out on my own couple of times. Once I was out there for ten days, and didn't speak. It does interesting things to the mind.

You have to go really early, like 5 a.m., before it gets too hot. If you can find somewhere that's a little bit shady near the mountains you can go in the afternoon, be on your own and have a little bit of a sleep. When it gets cooler you can walk around. Occasionally you get to see coyotes and roadrunners – just like the cartoon! But make sure that you get home before it gets dark or you're really screwed!

SIMIAN/
ALEX MacNAUGHTON
Holiday in Cyprus

192 <<   The place that I remember really fondly is sitting in a tent with my girlfriend on this amazing beach in the north of Cyprus. We were on holiday for a week, driving around by car. As soon as we found this beach, we stopped moving and stayed there for the rest of the week. I remember  one moment particularly, when we were both lying next to each other looking out of the tent and it was just a beautiful day. There was a beach a little bit further on and a little bar, where we could buy drinks.

The whole place was covered in tall eucalyptus trees which shed their leaves all over the ground. Because there were so many of them, the leaves had to be collected and burned. The smell of the burning leaves was just amazing.

THE FEATURES/
ROLLUM HAAS &
MATT PELHAM
Bottom Picture

We were at a club in Wales called The Butterfly and our manager got a little drunk and decided to take a picture of his own butt in the restroom. And then Parrish Yaw, our  194 <<
keyboardist, came in and caught him in the act and decided to take a picture of him taking a picture of his own butt. And that's the story!

I wanted to make a t-shirt out of the two pictures, one on the front of the shirt and one on the back. But I guess we were kind and didn't do it. We could have used it against him pretty happily, but we have been nice about it, except for things like this. Now it's finally exposed...

THE DANDY WARHOLS/
COURTNEY TAYLOR-TAYLOR
Stoned Impression

196 << I left some pot buried in a sidewalk
plant in front of a hotel in Canada.
This is sort of my impression of that
experience...

VEGA 4/
SIMON WALKER
Thoughts While Touring

198 << I thought I'd draw the inside of my head,
which is the place where I am all the time.
It's just a mix of thoughts, ideas, music
and melodies; also love, friendship and all
these neverending questions and answers
going around in there. This is the place I
can never escape from until I die, and the
things that go through my head nearly every day –
my favourite bands, movies, people I really care about,
things around me, what I see, what I hear, what I believe
in. In a band you travel around a lot and you get to see a
lot of different stuff. It makes you change your opinion a
lot and enlightens you.

I'll read out some of the words: escapism, growing up,
communication, laughter, health, love, God, friends,
happy, sad, sex – this is written very bold! – habits,
frequency, boredom – I suffered from that when I was
a kid – questions and answers. Sometimes you wonder
where ideas come from – it's like an antenna, picking up

things out of what you hear and see. The main thing that I have written is 'chaos', because that's what's in my head every day. It's like a big bowl of confusion, a traffic jam of thoughts and ideas. There are also words that refer to me personally, like moody, fun, happy. I put a question mark after the word 'happy', because I don't know what it's like to be really happy. I am happy, but not constantly. Some people are happy their entire lives.

MAROON 5/
JAMES VALENTINE
Bill

Los Angeles is our hometown. It's littered with people who moved there for acting and music, but who haven't made it. So there is always a kind of desperate quality about it. We have been on tour for the last two years and immediately I was drawn to Los Angeles, because we all miss it.

200 <<

The figure I have drawn I've called Bill. He could be just someone at the beach, but the more I think about it, he could represent me. He could be me in the future, because Bill has a kind of pathetic desperation in his eyes from having never really achieved his dreams, which is what Los Angeles is all about. I'm from Nebraska, so I am one of the people who came to L.A. to chase my dreams. I don't feel like Bill right now, but I am afraid of becoming him. Hopefully I never will.

The beach in L.A. is the place where people go to socialize. I've drawn litter on the beach, which is also a statement of our band's strong environmentalism and desire for cleaner beaches, water and air.

WIR SIND HELDEN/
JUDITH HOLOFERNES &
MARK TAVASSOL
Red Telephones

202 <<   This picture shows two different
places, symbolically divided by a
crack. On the left is Iran, on the
right is Germany. The scene is from
early 2002. In Germany there was a

band called 'Helden', but it wasn't yet complete. There
was also a bass player called 'Wir Sind', who was
actually me, Mark, but at the time I was in Iran, where I
come from. Pola from Helden was an old friend of mine
and suggested me as a bass player for the band. The
other three members didn't have any better ideas, so
they called me up in Iran and asked me to bring my 'Wir
Sind' over to make their band complete. The offer created
a huge dilemma in my life. Shortly before that, I had
accepted a job at a hospital and had signed a contract
with them. But I made my decision and the rest is
history.

On the German half of the picture, which was drawn
by me, Judith, you can see our side of the dilemma.
We were very much aware of the problems that our offer
had created for Mark. You can see weird little camels
roaming across the picture, bringing the two sides
together, and you can see our thought bubbles. In Jean's
bubble there's a hard disk recorder. This was the
artificial bass player we had in the band before, but it
was shit and we wanted to get rid of it. I'm imagining a
real bass, which looks a bit like an angel's harp in the
picture. And Pola's very optimistic thought bubble shows
the four of us together with our arms around each other,
relying on and supporting each other. We're also taking
a bow – the readers will have to imagine that part.
Anyway, our crazy idea worked out in the end. The
picture is also full of red telephone receivers, which
highlight the urgency of the situation.

This is the shed where we formed the band in 1992. It's an old derelict college in the countryside, beside my parents' house in Downpatrick. There are a lot of sentimental  204 << recollections there for us. It's where we wrote all our songs and where Ash started.

We used to rehearse there every Saturday until we were all about eighteen and we left Northern Ireland. We were playing for about two years as Ash before we got signed, so we were based in the shed for quite a long time. While we were playing, the plaster from the ceiling would crumble and fall down around us. And in the winter it was really cold. We had a heater going the whole time and we'd shiver and wish we could play with gloves on. We only had one plug so sometimes the heater blew up. That was difficult, because we would be kind of stuck, since it was the only place we could play without pissing everyone off.

Eventually we had to leave our rehearsal shed, because one day someone complained about the noise. For quite a while there weren't any houses nearby, so no one was really upset about it. The nearest people were across the river, but they had to cross the river to get us.

The shed is getting more and more run-down. One of these days it'll fall down. Right now it's a store for my parents' junk. We went back there in 1999 and 2000 to write Free All Angels. That was great, because it got us back to our roots – back to where we started.

NADA SURF/
IRA ELLIOT
Shut Up, Kids!

206 << This is the basement of the house in
Queens, New York, where I grew up.
We converted this room into a proper
music room. We covered the walls
with cheap yellow foam to keep the

noise down and we had an upright piano that we got
from somewhere. I rehearsed there with my first bands,
wrote songs and learned Aerosmith covers.

In 1979, when I was about fifteen, I was obsessed with
The Police. They were my favourite band and specially as
a drummer I was really into them. So I had a police
barricade and I'd take anything that had the word
'police' on it and I would collect any money that I had to
buy badges, t-shirts or Police fanzines. I was out of my
mind, I was crazy! I had this room till I was eighteen
years old. In this room I learned so much about music.
I listened to Led Zeppelin and Billy Joel, and I had a big
radio with a pair of headphones. So I just went from
station to station, and if I heard an Eagles song for
example, I would play it.

That was how I spent my spare time, listening to the
radio and playing along. I spent so much time in there
and I can't believe that my mom or the neighbours never
complained. Until one afternoon I was rehearsing with
an entire band and we were playing Ramones covers and
we got a phone call saying 'Shut up, kids!' So we turned
the music up and we all kept playing in the true spirit
of The Ramones. We had a lot of fun there. It was really
a fun place to be. I never went out – I just stayed
down there, pounding on the drums and driving the
neighbourhood crazy. I was encouraged all the time by
my parents and it was so easy for me. I was always
the one in the band who got this strong positive
reinforcement from everyone!

I didn't really think about my future at that point of my life, and I'm still not good at thinking about my future that much. But as soon as I was fifteen years old it was a kind of immediate gratification, because I was so much in love with playing. I was playing in local bands and with guys that I knew from the neighbourhood. So that was the beginning of the obsession, learning how to be in a band and dealing with bizarre personalities. I played in this room by myself for quite a number of years and you really can't learn about how to be a musician like that. You can put on headphones and listen to a record, that's one thing, but you really don't learn until you've got other people in the room and you have to give and take. You have to fit into the bigger picture.

THE HIVES/
PELLE ALMQVIST
Rehearsal Room & Disco in Sweden

This is the original 'Hives Manor'. It's a house that we borrowed, where we rehearsed and lived for a couple of years when we were touring and rehearsing. We eventually got

208 <<

evicted because the house was sold, and we had only borrowed it anyway! It was a pretty old house with three floors with quite a few rooms.

Even when we took the biggest room, it was hard for us to rehearse because it was pretty small, but it sounded great. There was a lot of good stuff happening. There was a tower where we could stand and look out over the sea. It was very nice to get that for free! There also used to be a big garage that was separate from the house and actually had a tenant living in it. He was a weird old guy who was a friend of the landlord. The rest of it was rented out to people with cars. And we would drive up this way in our white van when we were done with touring. There was a bar/discotheque thing right next to the manor, and we could hear the music through the wall. We could steal disco basslines because that's all we could hear. We heard the beats and then we spilt them up and made them into our own songs!

A river ran next to it and there was also a retirement home. I've drawn drunken people falling out of the disco and lying there – it must be a Saturday night! And some rubble, because nobody cleaned up the yard so it looks like a haunted house, which we thought was nice.

The house still exists. There is a family living in it now and they destroyed it by renovating it. We still pass by it every now and again, and sometimes when we are out in the country we have dinner there, because it's been turned into a restaurant. We haven't actually moved that far and still live close by. We've bought a new 'Hives Manor' now, but we still think of this as the original one. We once had a plan that we would all live there, but we quickly figured out that we were living with each other all the time when we were on tour anyway.

THE BLUESKINS/
RYAN SPENDLOVE
Lighthouse

210 <<

There's a village near Leeds called Garforth, where we spend four days a week practising throughout the day. So that's where everything comes from. Whatever we play as we go around the world, it's usually been first created in Garforth. Two hundred feet away there's a tower that we can see from our rehearsal room. When we came home from touring, that was one of the first things that we'd see. We knew we were home then, that we were safe! Our rehearsal room is like a community centre – a little hall that used to be a chapel. One of our friend's grandmothers used to own it. It's also close to where we live, right on our doorsteps, which is ideal! We thought the place was haunted because weird things happened, like strange noises and stuff falling over. We're used to it now, but when our friends come, they are really freaked out.

HOWIE
DAY
Party at a Lodge in the Woods

212 <<

This is my family's camping lodge down at a lake in Maine. It's about fifteen minutes out of Bangor where I live. So it's pretty close to a town, but it feels very isolated and in the middle of nowhere. I drew it at night because at night it's the most fun. You feel very isolated, partying with your friends in the dark. So the only thing that's warm in the picture is the lodge and everything else is in the dark. It's kind of scary! You can see some trees and rocks and the edge of the lake... and the man in the moon! I wasn't sure whether I should draw it in summer or in winter, because in winter the lake freezes and you can go ice-skating. I still look forward to going there. Just today I thought 'Man, I just can't wait to go there again! The summer is coming!'

THIRTEEN SENSES/
TOM WELHAM
Summertime

214 << This is a little beach where I grew up. When I was young, we spent most summers there and I used to go surfing. There's a lifeboat station, a little pier that's just behind it and

there's a beach tucked in there... In the middle there's a promenade with rocks. We actually tried to play a gig down by the beach, but we couldn't do it, because it's too expensive.

SONS AND DAUGHTERS/
SCOTT PATERSON
Strange Childhood Dream

I was born in Saudi Arabia and lived
over there when I was very young.
Then when I was six years old, I
came back to Scotland and lived in a
place called Cumbernauld, which is

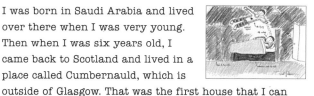

216 <<

outside of Glasgow. That was the first house that I can
remember living in. I used to have my own bedroom
there – it was before my brother was born – and I used to
have recurring dreams. Not unpleasant, not nightmares:
they were quite nice dreams.

I used to imagine I'd wake up and there would be a little
white star-shaped thing floating in front of me. I'd get up
and try to touch it and I would be kind of floating. I
couldn't see anything, but I felt like invisible hands were
holding me up. I'd float out of my bed and out of the
bedroom door, then down the stairs to the front door. I'd
be really slow and calm. I'd get to the front door, but I'd
never ever go out of it – I'd always wake up. I always
wanted the dream to continue so that I could go outside
and fly, but it never ever happened. I think I wore
Spiderman pyjamas…. oh, so bad! (laughs) There was a
door in my room, which led into a kind of attic space,
where we kept my dad's stuff. It was always very dark
and at that age you get very scared of the dark and
things. So I used to think there were monsters hiding in
there and monsters under the bed!

DIE TÜREN/
MAURICE SUMMEN
Fear of the Devil

218 <<   This is a dream that I often had
           when I was about six to eight years
           old. From my tree you can see
           bushes and behind every bush a little
           devil is hiding. Because of my Roman

Catholic upbringing, I was very scared of the Devil. This
dream only recurred during my childhood, never later. I
was scared of the dream as a child and then I got even
more scared.

I first had this dream around the same time as I had my
first wet dream. It was my guilty conscience that made
the devils appear. Then the devils wouldn't leave me
alone and followed me everywhere. Sometimes I dreamed
about running into a forest and getting lost. Along my
path I kept finding bushes, and all of them had a devil
lurking behind them. Now I only have a very hazy
recollection of it, but when I was asked to draw this
picture, it all came back to me.

SIMIAN/
SIMON LORD
Firework Battle

This is Bethesda, a small place in
North Wales near Bangor. It's a tiny
little place amid huge mountains,
and it's an old mining village, but
the mines are mostly shut now. We

220 <<

were staying in an old farmhouse with a studio in it, and
we were recording some b-sides for 'Mr Crow' and also
shooting a video. It was a really beautiful place with lots
of old forests. There was moss on the ground and a
really nice ambience about it. One evening a bunch of us
had a firework battle across the field, where we each had
ten firework rockets. It was really fun, kind of childish,
but we had a great time. It was like being in a gang,
doing stupid things together.

Bethesda's not the sort of place you just come across,
because it's so far away from everything, in the middle
of nowhere. But we've found out that quite a few
musicians in Welsh bands come from there, like Gorky's
Zygotic Mynci and Super Furry Animals. It's quite
renowned as the psychedelic centre of Wales. Lots of
strange and weird stories come from there. I can imagine
going back one day, if I just wanted to relax.

ABOUT THIS BOOK

Noel Gallagher pauses for a moment when we hand him the paper and pens. Then he vanishes backstage and comes back with a breadbasket. When we give him a questioning look at this peculiar object, he grins and puts the basket down on the sheet of paper that we've just given him. Suddenly we see what he wanted it for: the basket makes a perfect template for a smiley face! Noel draws around the circular basket and then carefully colours it bright yellow, while he tells us all about his life. He doesn't pause in his work until the pen starts to run out.

Our thoughts tend to consist of pictures rather than concepts, so we are all constantly creating images of things. Our memories store an enormous wealth of impressions, created by the endless stream of our perceptions and feelings. At first everything hits us at once, unordered and confusing, but over time these impressions are shaped into images. Most people try putting these images down on paper when they are at school, but many never do it again after that. We were therefore amazed by how positively musicians reacted when we asked them to draw or doodle a memorable place. Almost everyone we asked was keen to jot down their experiences and impressions in visual form. Many felt that drawing a picture took them back to the place itself, and they remembered details that they thought they'd forgotten. A few even described a personal experience that they had never talked about in an interview before.

It's usually very difficult to describe a place to someone in such a way that they can build up their own rough image of what it's like. Even if you use a photo to help you, it's often impossible without additional explanations. Without visual references, people tend to come up with a different interpretation of their own. This image often has very little in common with the original impression of the place that the speaker is trying to describe. The full picture exists only inside their head.

The question of how important a place is to someone can only be answered by that particular person. Nonetheless, it's interesting to find out why and to what extent musicians identify with particular locations. Do they perhaps have a completely different grasp on what 'home' means? After all, they are always on the move.

For most 'normal' people, travelling is something special, not an everyday occurrence. Musicians, on the other hand, are almost always on the road as soon as they've made it big. They don't just want their music to be listened to, they want to play it live too.

What bands remember most about a tour and what impressions they bring home with them is a subject that hasn't been examined very closely. What images and experiences stay with them? How do they describe touring? Does touring still feel special even if they're doing it constantly?

Different bands get different impressions, and this can be clearly seen when you look at their lyrics. Finnish band The Crash were dreaming of the glamour of the Big Apple when they wrote 'New York', but Interpol's 'NYC' casts a much more critical eye over the city. Art Brut's song 'Moving to L.A.' shows that even rock stars dream of escaping from the British weather and heading for the sunshine of California, although the dream tends to be more accessible to them than it is for the average fan.

Maxïmo Park's 'The Coast Is Always Changing' talks of of the dissatisfaction of staying still and the happiness of constantly being on the move and looking for something new. Athlete's 'El Salvador', meanwhile, describes how distanced it's possible to feel from your own life, which can seem to be moving on independently of you.

At the very beginning, we decided to make this project as simple as possible. The same tools were given to all the bands: one sheet of drawing paper, plus pencils, felt-tip pens and wax crayons. With this equipment, they had to try their hands at being visual artists, wherever they happened to be at the time. Some produced their works of art in the shelter of the tour bus, others on park benches, some on darkened stages after a gig and some on dim street corners.

Most people reacted to our unusual request in an amazingly positive way. For example, Kelly Jones of Stereophonics called off an interview with a journalist from one of the largest German music magazines, preferring a chance to be creative to the thought of answering the same old questions. He wasn't the only one who was bored with traditional interviews and who welcomed the opportunity to do something different. Often the drawing session would begin and soon afterwards, all the band members would be busy with their paper and pens. Our sketch collection grew and grew. Nicky Wire of the Manic Street Preachers unfortunately wasn't able to meet us personally, but he didn't let that stop him from taking part: shortly after we'd made our request, a courier delivered an oil painting by Wire right to our door.

We didn't get such a positive response from everyone that we approached, however. Back at the very start of the project, out of purely experimental interest and to keep a PR girl happy, we met up with the guys from Right Said Fred, but they wouldn't pick up a pen until we let them have a financial cut of the project. Fortunately not just for us, but for the music business as a whole and indeed for anyone with ears, there are plenty of bands around who are not Right Said Fred.

The music business is often less to do with art and more with commerce, but hindsight we are grateful that priorities on the indie and alternative scene tend to be different. Our special thanks go to Paul Smith of Maxïmo Park, who wrote the foreword, and to everyone else who took part in our project.

Silke Leicher & Manuel Schreiner

BANDS AND ARTISTS

AQUALUNG   Matt Hales grew up in Southampton where his parents ran a record shop, and went on to study music composition. After some unsuccessful attempts with bands, he started recording under the name Aqualung, and his single 'Strange and Beautiful' became a UK hit after being featured in a TV ad for the Volkswagen Beetle. This was followed by an eponymous debut album.

ART BRUT   This Bournemouth band take their name from an art movement first described in the late 1940s by Jean Dubuffet, which embraces works created by psychiatric patients and other social outsiders. The raw, unrefined nature of those works of art is a source of inspiration to singer Eddie Argos.

ASH   Tim Wheeler (vocals, guitar), Mark Hamilton (bass) and Rick McMurray (drums) were schoolmates from Downpatrick, Northern Ireland. They were later joined by Charlotte Hatherley as a second guitarist. Their breakthrough came in 1995 with the singles 'Kung Fu' and 'Girl From Mars'.

ATHLETE   Hailing from Deptford in London, the band name among their musical influences The Flaming Lips, Pavement and Stevie Wonder. Their debut album *Vehicles and Animals* was nominated for the Mercury Prize in 2003.

MELISSA AUF DER MAUR   Daughter of a journalist and a translator, she attended FACE School for the Performing Arts in Montreal where she studied piano, trumpet and choral singing, before majoring in photography at Concordia University. She was the bassist with Hole before touring with The Smashing Pumpkins and later releasing a solo album, featuring backing from members of Queens of the Stone Age.

BABYSHAMBLES After being thrown out of The Libertines due to his substance misuse problems, Pete Doherty established Babyshambles, who combine lyrical elegance with wild energy. To the public at large Doherty is probably better known as the former boyfriend of Kate Moss than for his musical endeavours.

BELLE AND SEBASTIAN Glasgow band who take their name from a children's book by Cécile Aubry that became a 1960s TV series. Bassist Stuart David left the band and became a novelist himself, writing *Nalda Said* and *The Peacock Manifesto*. Stuart Murdoch's songs, often inspired by characters from the Scottish indie scene, are a match for any book.

BLACK REBEL MOTORCYCLE CLUB San Francisco trio named after Marlon Brando's biker gang from the movie *The Wild One*, and influenced by psychedelic rock, garage rock and punk. Their 2005 album *Howl* paid tribute to the Beat poet Allen Ginsberg and their Californian roots.

BLOC PARTY London band formed in 1998 under the name The Angel Range, and influenced by Sonic Youth, Joy Division, Gang of Four and The Cure. Their debut *Silent Alarm* was named Album of the Year in 2005 by the *NME*.

THE BLUESKINS Four-piece band from the Wakefield area, formed in 1999. Before their pure rock'n'roll with soul came along, nights out in Wakefield meant getting drunk and getting into fights. Influenced by a love of Led Zeppelin, Bob Marley and punk, their debut single was championed by John Peel.

BRITISH SEA POWER Brighton band signed by Rough Trade boss Geoff Lewis. Their debut album won plaudits from David Bowie, Lou Reed and Radiohead and they were also praised by Jarvis Cocker, who said that their music gave him the feeling of looking out over valleys, lake and forests.

CAESARS Swedish band formerly known as Caesars Palace, who shortened their name to avoid confusion with the famous Las Vegas casino. Their mix of Beatles-style melodies, Beach Boys harmonies and psychedelia impressed Apple, who featured their song 'Jerk It Out' on an iPod commercial.

CLIENT Electronic group formed by Sarah Blackwood, former singer of Dubstar, and Kate Holmes, wife of Alan McGee, the founder of Creation Records. Originally the band members remained anonymous, using only the nicknames Client A and Client B. They have toured with Depeche Mode and recorded a track with Pete Doherty.

COLDPLAY British band who first met at University College London in 1996. They have won multiple Grammys and MTV awards for their albums *Parachutes* and *A Rush of Blood to the Head*. Singer Chris Martin's marriage to actress Gwyneth Paltrow has made them as much of a fixture in the tabloids as in the music press.

THE COOPER TEMPLE CLAUSE Originally a six-piece from Berkshire, they began rehearsing in a former pig farm near Reading. Their output was influenced by prog rock, Britpop and electronica. Bassist Didz Hammond left to join Dirty Pretty Things in 2005, and the rest of the band finally split in April 2007.

THE CORAL Formed in Hoylake in the Wirral in 1996, the band first met at school. They started out playing Oasis covers, but ended up supporting Oasis themselves and recording in Noel Gallagher's studio. Their self-titled debut album was nominated for the Mercury Prize in 2002.

COSMIC CASINO Munich-based five-piece indie band who sing in English and prefer to let their live shows speak for themselves. They have played support for Stereophonics, The Hives, Mother Tongue and Slut, among others.

THE CRASH Formed in Turku in 1991, they have become one of Finland's biggest musical exports after The Leningrad Cowboys, The Rasmus and HIM. Their song 'Star' was used by eBay on its European commercials.

THE DANDY WARHOLS Formed in Portland, Oregon, in 1992 by glam rock fan Courtney Taylor-Taylor and guitarist Peter Holmstrom: the two first met at the age of fourteen at a music summer camp. Their psychedelic style brings together influences as diverse as Duran Duran and The Velvet Underground.

THE DATSUNS Under the name Trinket, the band won a local radio Battle of the Bands contest in their native Cambridge, New Zealand, in 1999. In 2000 they renamed themselves The Datsuns and started to play Ramones-influenced hard rock with plenty of guitar solos.

HOWIE DAY Born in 1981 in Bangor, Maine (the hometown of Stephen King), Howie Day was fifteen when he played his first gig. Winner of two Boston Music Awards, he often builds his stage performances around live sampling and improvisation. 'Sometimes, something great will come out of it, but on other nights it might all be garbage.'

DEATH CAB FOR CUTIE Formed in Bellingham, Washington, in 1997 by student Benjamin Gibbard, and named after a song by the Bonzo Dog Doo-Dah Band, this indie rock band came to prominence when their music was featured on the hit US TV series *The O.C.*

DELAYS Brothers Greg and Aaron Gilbert met Colin Fox and Rowly at school in Southampton and all shared a love of music. Their 2004 debut album showcased their distinctive falsetto vocal sound and led to support slots with bands including Franz Ferdinand and Manic Street Preachers.

THE DETROIT COBRAS Retro-garage band who specialize in covers of classic and rediscovered rock songs. Their line-up changes frequently but singer Rachel Nagy and guitarist Maribel Restrepo remain the band's driving force. Their video for 'Cha Cha Twist' featured a guest appearance by Meg White of The White Stripes as Little Red Riding Hood.

DIRTY PRETTY THINGS When Pete Doherty left The Libertines, the remaining band members formed Dirty Pretty Things, along with Didz Hammond, formerly of The Cooper Temple Clause. Their debut album *Waterloo to Anywhere* was well received and their first single 'Bang Bang You're Dead' became a top five hit in the UK.

CRISTINA DONÀ Italian singer-songwriter, known for her voyages into fantastic realms of sound. Her voice seems fragile and delicate but can be unexpectedly powerful. She collaborated with Robert Wyatt on her album *Dove sei tu*.

THE DRESDEN DOLLS Expressive vocals and unusual keyboards are the musical hallmarks of Amanda Palmer and Brian Viglione. These Boston-based admirers of Kurt Weill and Patti Smith produce a bewitching and theatrical mix of punk and cabaret.

EMBRACE Yorkshire band formed by brothers Danny and Richard McNamara, who released their first album *The Good Will Out* in 1998. Known for their Britpop anthems, but not afraid to experiment: their song 'Hooligan' notably features a kazoo solo.

ESKOBAR Swedish indie band formed in 1994, hailing from the small town of Åkersberga and led by heartthrob singer Daniel Bellqvist. Their melancholy, emotional but simply arranged songs recall the work of Chris Isaak.

THE FEATURES Matt Pelham (guitar and vocals), Roger Dabbs (bass) and Parrish Yaw (keyboards) first formed a band in Sparta, Tennessee, at the age of thirteen. They continued to play through high school and absorbed influences from Bob Dylan and The Beastie Boys.

FEEDER After their 1997 album *Polythene* was named Album of the Year by *Metal Hammer*, the South Wales trio took the hard rock scene by storm. Shortly after the release of their 2001 album *Echo Park*, their drummer Jon Lee sadly took his own life in January 2002. Mark Richardson, formerly of Skunk Anansie, was brought in as a replacement drummer.

FRANZ FERDINAND Acclaimed Scottish new wave band, named after the former Archduke of Austria whose assassination by a Serbian terrorist triggered the First World War. The band's self-titled debut album won the Mercury Prize in 2004 and was named *NME's* Album of the Year.

FUCK Indie-pop four-piece founded in 1993 in Oakland, California, after its members met in a police holding cell. The band's name often appears in a censored form on album covers and gig posters, for obvious reasons.

ADAM GREEN Soft-voiced singer-songwriter whose twisted lyrics about drugs and relationships have made him a pillar of the anti-folk scene. Formerly the singer with The Moldy Peaches, he has also recorded poetry, and describes himself as the type of person who can spend days at a time watching old movies and eating takeaway pizza.

HAL Irish four-piece centred around brothers Dave and Paul Allen, and named after the computer in *2001: A Space Odyssey*. Their retro harmonies first attracted the attention of a record label after a series of monthly gigs at The Sugar Club in Dublin.

THE HIVES Swedish band with mod and punk influences, who claim to have been founded in 1993 by the mysterious figure of Randy Fitzsimmons, allegedly their songwriter and manager. They are known for their matching suits in stark black and white, and for vocalist Pelle Almqvist's on-stage showmanship.

HOOBASTANK Los Angeles band who first got together in 1994. When asked what the band's name meant, singer Doug Robb explains that it was 'one of those old high school inside-joke words that didn't really mean anything'. Finnish-born bassist Markku Lappalainen left in 2005 and was replaced by Josh Moreau.

I AM KLOOT Trio from Manchester who met in 1999 in a club where singer and guitarist John Bramwell worked as a booker. Their debut album *Natural History* showcased their darkly witty love songs and put them at the forefront of the 'quiet is the new loud' scene.

IDLEWILD Founded in Edinburgh in 1996 by four students who met at a party and realized they had the same musical tastes. They've played support for Coldplay and Pearl Jam, and their rough surface hides a surprisingly delicate interior.

THE (INTERNATIONAL) NOISE CONSPIRACY
Dennis Lyzén sang in the band Refused before forming The (International) Noise Conspiracy in Umeå, Sweden in 1998. They combine radically political lyrics with punk-influenced music. In the studio they have collaborated with producer Rick Rubin and keyboardist Billy Preston.

INTERPOL Post-punk band who formed in 1998 at New York University. They have talked of wanting their music to be a similar experience to seeing a great movie. *Turn on the Bright Lights* was one of the *NME*'s top ten albums of 2002.

JJ72 Indie band from Dublin, formed in 1999 by singer Mark Greaney and drummer Fergal Matthews. Bassist Hilary Woods was once named sexiest woman in rock by *Melody Maker*. The band split in June 2006.

KAISER CHIEFS Leeds-based five-piece who burst onto the music scene in 2005 with their debut album *Employment*, which was subsequently nominated for the Mercury Prize. They have since built up a reputation for their live shows and have won multiple BRIT and *NME* awards, including singer Ricky Wilson being named as Best Dressed of 2006.

KASABIAN Band from Leicester who took their name from Linda Kasabian, a member of Charles Manson's cult 'The Family'. The music press often compares them to 'Madchester' bands such as The Stone Roses, although they dispute this tag as 'lazy journalism'. They were named Best Live Act of 2007 by the *NME*.

KEANE From the town of Battle in East Sussex, the band first got together in 1996 and took their current name from Cherry Keane, a late friend of Tom Chaplin's mother. Their bittersweet melodies have won them BRIT and Q Awards. An *NME* review once described them as sounding like '*Kid A*-era Radiohead covering A-ha'.

THE KILLERS Post-punk/alternative band from Las Vegas fronted by charismatic singer Brandon Flowers. Their name comes from a fictional band portrayed in the video for 'Crystal' by New Order, which the Killers paid tribute to in their own video for the huge international hit 'Somebody Told Me'.

JEFFREY LEWIS Discordant guitars and complex, witty lyrics are the hallmarks of this New York anti-folk singer and comic-book artist, who follows in the footsteps of Allen Ginsberg and The Fugs. Mumbled vocals and lo-fi sounds recall the bohemian zeitgeist of the 1960s.

THE LIBERTINES Formed in 1997 by Carl Barât and Pete Doherty, The Libertines were critically acclaimed as a new wave of Britpop. Known for their on- and off-stage excesses, the band split in 2004, due predominantly to Doherty's on-going drug problems. Doherty and Barât are now focused on separate projects, but they did perform live together in 2007.

LIFE OF AGONY Alternative metal band from Brooklyn, New York, first formed in 1989. Their 1993 debut, *River Runs Red*, was a concept album about a high-school student who contemplates and eventually commits suicide. They split in 1999 but later reunited, culminating in their 2005 album *Broken Valley*.

LOUIS XIV Named after a 17th-century French king, this San Diego band formed in 2003, having known each other since childhood. Inspired by the likes of T-Rex, David Bowie and AC/DC, they combine glam rock, seventies-style guitars and double-entendre-filled lyrics.

MANDO DIAO The industrial town of Borlänge in Sweden is home to rock band Mando Diao, whose striking but meaningless name came to singer Björn Dixgård in a dream. They formed in 1999, but their 2004 album *Hurricane Bar* was the first to make an international impression.

MANIC STREET PREACHERS After their guitarist and lyricist Richey Edwards went missing in 1995, this Welsh rock band successfully continued as a three-piece and went on to win multiple BRIT and Q Awards. Bassist Nicky Wire took over lyric-writing duties for their intelligent, politically conscious songs.

MAROON 5 Formerly known as Kara's Flowers, the band fronted by Adam Levine played their first gig at the Whisky a-Go-Go in L.A. in 1995. Their first album failed to take off, and Levine moved to New York where he was influenced by hip-hop, R&B and funk. The band reformed under the name Maroon 5 and their debut album, *Songs About Jane*, sealed their international success.

JOHNNY MARR Born in 1963 in Ardwick, Manchester, to Irish parents, Marr rose to fame in the 1980s as guitarist and co-songwriter of The Smiths. Since leaving the band in 1987 he has recorded and toured with many other musicians, ranging from Bryan Ferry and Beck to the Pretenders and the Pet Shop Boys. In 2006 he became full-time guitarist with US band Modest Mouse.

MAXÏMO PARK Five-piece band from the north-east of England, who take their name from Maximo Gomez Park in Havana, a one-time meeting place for revolutionaries. Their 2005 debut *A Certain Trigger* was nominated for the Mercury Prize and they are known for their wild and energetic live shows.

MONEYBROTHER The solo project of Swedish musician Anders Wendin, former singer in the ska-punk band Monster. The Moneybrother sound is soul-influenced pop/rock, with Wendin's vocals often compared to Joe Strummer or Bruce Springsteen.

MUSE Devon band formed in 1994. Frontman Matthew Bellamy's eccentric lyrics combine with the backing of drummer Dominic Howard and bassist Christopher Wolstenholme to create dynamic stage performances and a sound that develops with each new album. Their 2006 release *Black Holes & Revelations* was nominated for the Mercury Prize.

NADA SURF New York band whose distinctive songs about love, rage and fruit flies have often been viewed with confusion by US record companies. Their first album *High/Low* was produced by Ric Ocasek and spawned their biggest homeland hit, 'Popular', but their more recent releases have found a following in Europe and elsewhere.

OASIS Leading lights of the early 1990s Britpop movement, the Manchester band formed by brothers Noel and Liam Gallagher have sold more than 50 million albums worldwide, with *Definitely Maybe* in 1994 becoming the fastest-selling debut album of all time in the UK.

OCEAN COLOUR SCENE Although they formed back in 1989, this Birmingham band's breakthrough came with their 1996 album *Moseley Shoals*. The follow-up, *Marchin' Already*, was also a huge hit, reaching number one in the UK album charts. Their admirers include Paul Weller and the Gallagher brothers, who named them the 'second best band in Britain'.

OCEANSIZE Manchester-based band formed in the early 2000s and named after the track 'Ocean Size' by Jane's Addiction. Their music has been called progressive, a label that they formerly fought against but have since come to accept to a certain degree.

PHOENIX Indie electronica band formed in Versailles, France, in 1991. They appeared as a backing group for Air before releasing their own debut album in 2000. Film director Sofia Coppola is a fan, and featured their music in the movie *Lost In Translation*.

THE RACONTEURS Collaborative band including Jack White, taking time out from The White Stripes, Jack Lawrence and Patrick Keeler of The Greenhornes, and Brendan Benson. Their music brings the raw minimalism of White and the poppier influences of Benson together with a bluesier edge. In 2006 *Broken Boy Soldiers* was named album of the year by *Mojo* magazine.

THE SHINS They began as a side project for singer and guitarist James Mercer of Flake Music but soon became a notable outfit in their own right and were signed when Jonathan Poneman of the grunge label Sub Pop saw them playing in San Francisco.

SIMIAN Jas Shaw and Alex MacNaughton were childhood friends who played in various folk-rock bands in Kent before forming Simian while at Manchester University. The band split in 2005 but Shaw and James Ford continue to work as producers and remixers under the name Simian Mobile Disco.

SLUT A German band who sing in English, Slut were formed in Ingolstadt, Bavaria, in the mid-1990s. Two of their songs feature on the soundtrack of the successful 2000 German movie *Crazy*. In 2005 they submitted the track 'Why Pourquoi?' as a potential German entry in the Eurovision Song Contest but failed to qualify.

SNOW PATROL Formed in 1995 in Dundee, Scotland, although most of the members hail from Northern Ireland, Snow Patrol's anthemic power pop has crossed over into mainstream success in recent years. *Eyes Open* was nominated as Best British Album at the 2007 BRIT Awards.

SONS AND DAUGHTERS Glasgow four-piece, two of whom were previously members of Arab Strap. Led by the charismatic Adele Bethel, they have supported Morrissey and Franz Ferdinand, and their 2008 album *This Gift* was produced by Bernard Butler.

THE SOUNDTRACK OF OUR LIVES As members of Swedish punk band Union Carbide Productions, singer Ebbot Lundberg and guitarist Ian Person indulged their love of Iggy Pop and the Stooges. After 'Sweden's most exciting rock'n'roll machine' split in the mid-1990s, they formed TSOOL and received a Grammy nomination for their album *Behind the Music*.

SPARTA The 2001 split of the US hardcore band At The Drive-In resulted in the formation of two new bands, of which Sparta were one and The Mars Volta the other. Sparta have since released three albums, their driving sound often uniting exuberance and despair.

SPEARMINT London-based band who formed in the mid-1990s. Their album *My Missing Days* took listeners through a backwards narrative, and their song 'Scottish Pop' paid tribute to many of their favourite artists. The *NME* called them one of the last great indie bands.

STARS The roots of Stars lie in New York, where Torquil Campbell was working as an actor, guest-starring in *Sex and the City* and *Law & Order*, and Chris Seligman was playing in the orchestra of a Broadway show. They decided to form their own band and moved back to Montreal in their native Canada.

STARSAILOR Band from Chorley in Lancashire, named after a Tim Buckley album. Singer and songwriter James Walsh, who 'wanted to do something that was really natural and says something about who you are and how you're feeling rather than just making a noise', first met James Stelfox (bass) and Ben Byrne (drums) at music college in Wigan.

STEREOPHONICS Kelly Jones, Richard Jones and Stuart Cable grew up together in the South Wales village of Cwmaman and began playing as a covers band in the early 1990s. In 1998 they were named Best New Act at the BRIT awards, and went on to have five number one albums in the UK. Cable was replaced by Argentinian Javier Weyler in 2003.

KEN STRINGFELLOW American guitarist best known as a member of White Flag and The Posies, and for his work with REM. His solo albums have featured such diverse influences as Joni Mitchell, Buffalo Springfield, and dub reggae.

SUGARPLUM FAIRY Band from the Swedish town of Borlänge, led by Victor and Carl Norén, the brothers of Gustav Norén from Mando Diao. They take their name from a recording of 'A Day In The Life' by the Beatles, in which John Lennon uses the words 'sugar-plum fairy' to count in the song.

TELE Founded in Freiburg, Germany, in the late 1990s but now based in Berlin, this five-piece produce danceable indie pop with German lyrics and have collaborated with other acclaimed German bands including Wir Sind Helden.

THIRTEEN SENSES Four-piece from Cornwall, led by singer-songwriter Will South, who grew up listening to the Beatles. Their 2004 debut album *The Invitation* was described as 'sumptuous shimmer-folk' by the *NME*.

THE THRILLS Daniel Ryan and Conor Deasy grew up as neighbours in Dublin and together with three schoolmates they formed the band which became The Thrills. They spent a summer together in California writing songs for their first album, *So Much for the City*. Marilyn Manson producer Dave Sardy produced their 2004 follow-up, *Let's Bottle Bohemia*.

... TRAIL OF DEAD Anthemic art rock band, based in Austin, Texas, who claim that their full name, ...And You Will Know Us By The Trail Of Dead, is taken from a Mayan ritual chant. Childhood friends Conrad Keely and Jason Reece take the creative lead.

TRAVIS Fran Healy (vocals), Andy Dunlop (guitar), Douglas Payne (bass) and Neil Primrose (drums) met as students in Glasgow in the early 1990s, and released their first single, 'All I Want To Do Is Rock', in 1996 with money from Healy's mother. Their breakthrough came with the album *The Man Who* in 1999, and they subsequently won several BRIT awards.

DIE TÜREN Berlin-based trash-punk trio with eighties influences. Their name means 'The Doors', although they claim they chose it because they wanted a meaningless-sounding name, and not as a reference to Jim Morrison's band.

THE USED Rock band from Orem, Utah, who formed in 2001, although several of its members had played together previously in local groups. Singer Bert McCracken famously dated Kelly Osbourne, daughter of Ozzy.

VEGA 4 London-based four-piece with an international line-up: Johnny McDaid and Gavin Fox are from Ireland, Bryan McLellan from Canada and Bruce Gainsford from New Zealand. They announced their split in early 2008.

THE VON BONDIES Following in the footsteps of The MC5 and The Stooges, The Von Bondies hail from Detroit. Jack White of The White Stripes produced their debut album and hired them to support him on a US and European tour.

WE ARE SCIENTISTS A US band whose members met at college in California, they take their name from a removal man who asked them if they were scientists. They have toured with Arctic Monkeys and Kaiser Chiefs, among others.

THE WEDDING PRESENT This Leeds band formed in the mid-eighties and found success on the indie scene after being championed by legendary DJ John Peel, who called David Gedge the writer of some of the best love songs of all time. After many line-up changes, the band were inactive for several years but Gedge reformed them in 2004.

WIR SIND HELDEN German synth-pop band whose name means 'We Are Heroes', led by singer and guitarist Judith Holofernes. In 2003 they were at the forefront of a new wave of bands who revitalized the German music scene.

2RAUMWOHNUNG Electronic duo from Berlin whose name means 'Two-Room Apartment', formed by Inga Humpe (formerly of Neonbabies) and Tommi Eckhart. They originally got together in 2000 to create music for a German cigarette commercial, but kept the band going when that track took off on the club scene and then became a chart hit.

This book would not have been possible without the following people:

Gavin Brady, Mirjam Kolb, Michael Scheuber, Stacey Sievewright, Oliver Srock

THANKS TO:

Our parents, Nils Andersen, Thomas B., Volker Banasiak, Nicole Bauroth, Oliver Bergmann, Karsten Braun, Thorsten Buhl, Nadin Brendel, Ralph Buchbender, Heide Buhmann, Dennis Dührkoop, Camilo Eytel, Jascha Farhangi, Christoph Faust & Velveteen, Sven Fiege-Brill, Paul Fells, Oliver Fennel, Yvonne Fischer, Ansgar Fleischmann, Michael Fuchs-Gamböck, Sven Geis, Simone Geldmacher, Liz Gould, Hanspeter Haeseler, Bernd Harbauer, Christoph Hein, Thomas Hessberger, Andrew Hill, Steffi Horstmüller, Carolin Jacob, Sandra Kinzelmann, Ole Kirchhoff, Christian Klabunde, Tina Koppelin, Imme Krain, Heidrun Kruse-Krebs, Maren Kumpe, Kerstin Lamb, Florian Lamp, Achim Launert, Günther Leicher, Michael Löffler, Heiko Mack, Hanns Christian Mahler, Klaus Mai, Denise Mayer, Claudia Medel, Meetz, Ute Miehling, Elena Nehrmann, Claudia Neufert, Nicky, Claudia Penzkofer, Andrew Quarterman, Simon Rass, Marcel Reckler, Jürgen Reichert, Birgit Schapow, Ulrike Schasse, Anke Schneider, Thomas Schreiber, Hollow Skai, Sven Städtler, Colette Stritzke, Martin Url, Stephan Velten, Klemens Wiese and to everyone else who supported this project, and anyone we forgot to mention!

Photos of the bands are reproduced by kind permission of: Sony/BMG, Rough Trade Records, Sanctuary Music, EMI Music, Capitol Records, Apricot Records, Virgin Records, Labels, V2 Records, Warner Music, Domino Records, City Slang, Cargo Records, Universal Music, Edel Music, PIAS Recordings, Beggars Banquet, Indigo, KOOK, Ryko, Roadrunner Records, SPV, Burning Heart, Sub Pop and Stickman.